A Geneva Series Commentary

ZECHARIAH

A
Commentary
on
ZECHARIAH

THOMAS V. MOORE, D.D.

"The Lord our God be with us, as he was with our fathers: let him not leave us, nor forsake us." 1 KINGS 8.57.

THE BANNER OF TRUTH TRUST
78b Chiltern Street, London, W.1.

Reprinted October 1958
,, October 1961

Printed in Gt. Britain by
Photo-Litho
PHOTOTYPE LTD., LONDON

PUBLISHERS' FOREWORD

A hundred years have passed since the first appearance of this commentary and it is now probably known to very few. It would therefore seem advisable to give some word of explanation with regard to the cause of its re-publication. There are a multitude of books which call for the time and consideration of Christians today and the serious believer who is concerned to redeem the time has every reason to ask what justification any work has for meriting his attention. The hours that most can give to reading are few and one is right in being concerned to study nothing but the best. With such thoughts in mind let us briefly consider this present work.

As an exposition of Scripture it has not become dated since its first publication, and despite a few philological advances that may have been made, the fact remains that no work on Zechariah has since appeared which combines such scholarship and devotion in a form which the ordinary believer is well able to follow. As a commentator Moore inherited much of the exegetical powers of Dr. J. A. Alexander—his tutor at Princeton Theological Seminary—and the first prerequisite of all sound exposition, that is deep Christian piety, is as prominent in his writings as it was in those of the Puritans. C. H. Spurgeon summarized the value of Moore's work in the highest terms, "A capital book", he wrote; "Most useful to Ministers". Such commentators are not to be found amongst us today.

If the first reason for commending this book is that it will lead the reader deeply into the Scriptures, the second is that it is dealing with a portion of God's Word which is vitally relevant to the present state of the Christian Church. No book in Scripture can better enable us to face our contemporary circumstances in the right manner than this one. The reason for this lies in the similarity between Zechariah's times and our own. The seventy years preceding the commencement of his ministry had been years of sad changes and judgments among God's people; the Church had languished in captivity, her prophets were removed from her, Zion was broken down and the glory of her former days departed, and the rebuilding of the temple had been begun but only to be brought to a standstill. Such was the situation in 520 B.C. or thereabouts when this prophecy opens. The Jews who had returned from exile were a discouraged remnant, ready in the face of so many obstacles and hindrances to give way to sloth, faint-heartedness and discouragement. The main design of Zechariah's prophecy is, therefore, to administer encouragement and instruction to the people of God who were in such a low condition. It is thus peculiarly adapted to strengthen the Church in every period of spiritual weakness and darkness, for the grounds on which Zechariah bases his exhortations are grounds which will remain in force till the end of time, and the promises of the final completion and prosperity of God's work will only be ultimately fulfilled in the second coming of Christ.

It is not surprising that this prophecy has always been of especial consolation to believers in times of struggle and temptation to despair. Luther and Calvin valued it highly and saw clearly its application to their own times. The great Reformer of Geneva in his commentary on this book, Chapter 4. v. 7 writes: "This doctrine may be fitly applied to our age: for we see how Satan raises up great forces, we see how the whole world conspires against the Church, to prevent the increase or the progress of the Kingdom of Christ. When we consider how great are the difficulties which meet us, we are ready to faint and to become wholly dejected. Let us then remember that it is no new thing for enemies to surpass great mountains in elevation; but that the Lord can at length reduce them to a plain. This, then, our shield can cast down and lay prostrate whatever greatness the devil may set up to terrify us: for as the Lord then reduced a great mountain to a plain, when Zerubbabel was able to do nothing, so at this day, however boldly multiplied adversaries may resist Christ in the work of building a spiritual temple to God the Father, yet all their efforts will be in vain."

It is a sad thing that this part of Scripture should be so little known today. Never was its message more needed, yet no adequate commentary on Zechariah appears to be in print in this country. We are therefore thankful to be able to make Moore's valuable work available again. It was first published along with commentaries on Haggai and Malachi under the title "The Prophets of the Restoration" and included a lengthy Introduction on the nature of Old Testament prophecy. What is here omitted from the original large volume may later be reprinted in separate form. After comparing this commentary with others on this prophecy that might have been selected for reprinting, we are satisfied in the rightness of this choice, and pray that it will again be widely used to serve the needs of the Church in these present times.

PREFACE.

A FEW words of explanation may not be improper in presenting this work to the public, for the sake of those who are willing to read a Preface.

The title, and some of the most valuable thoughts of the Introduction, were suggested to me by one whose aid I acknowledge with a gratitude that extends backward to the time when I had the rare privilege of listening to words of instruction both from his lips, and from those of his honored father, whose memory is cherished by all his pupils with the fondness of a child's affection for a beloved parent. I refer to the Rev. J. A. Alexander, D.D., to whom the church may hereafter be as largely indebted in the department of ecclesiastical history, if his life be spared, as it is now in that of exegesis.

I have in each successive revision of my studies used honestly every aid within my reach; and although, in the absorbing cares and duties of a large pastoral charge, I have not been able to bestow as much care on minute points as I might have done otherwise, I have endeavored to give every matter that had any important bear-

ing on the meaning of the text a full and impartial
consideration, and aimed to set forth simply and clearly
the mind of the Spirit.

I have given first my own translation, which is presented, like that of Newcome, Henderson, Calvin, and
others, in a metrical form, according to the parallelisms.
In the Exposition, I have repeated this translation in the
notes, that it might be more readily compared with the
English version that is given at the top of the page. I
have as much as possible avoided the introduction of Hebrew words into the notes, but it could not be avoided
at times without an awkward, if not unintelligible, peri-
phrasis. I have endeavored to avoid all unnecessary
expansion of such points as are purely homiletic
and practical, whilst I have endeavored to suggest
them in a way that may readily be followed out by those
who desire to pursue these themes at greater length.
My object has been to furnish such an exposition
of the meaning of the text as would be intelligible
to any thinking layman who wished to understand
the Scriptures thoroughly, and also to aid my brethren in the ministry, whose circumstances or studies
had not led them to any special investigation of these
portions of God's Word. If I have not fully succeeded
in combining these two things, those who understand
most of this subject will best understand the difficulty
of the task. But I can say in all sincerity, as the good
Bishop Horne did, in sending forth his Commentary on
the Psalms, that the work has been its own reward,

and that if any one shall experience half the pleasure in reading it that I did in writing it, my labor has not been misapplied. But I send it forth with the hope that God may bless this feeble effort to turn attention to His Holy Word, and induce other and abler hands to engage in the same blessed and self-rewarding employment. And if a Dedication were in good taste in such a work, I would respectfully and humbly dedicate it to that body of men, who are doing more for the world, and for whom the world is doing less in return, than any other class of workers in society—*my Brethren in the Christian Ministry.*

RICHMOND, VA., Jan. 1, 1856.

ZECHÁRIAH.

TRANSLATION.

PART I.—INTRODUCTION.

CHAPTER 1 : 1—6.

1: 1. In the eighth month, in the second year of Darius, came the
word of Jehovah unto Zechariah, son of Berechiah, son
of Iddo, the Prophet, saying,

2. 'Angry hath Jehovah been toward your fathers with
(*great*) anger.

3. Therefore say thou unto them,
Thus saith Jehovah of Hosts,
Return ye unto me,
Saith Jehovah of Hosts,
And I will return unto you,
Saith Jehovah of Hosts.

4. Be ye not as your fathers, unto whom the former prophets
cried saying,
Thus saith Jehovah of Hosts ;
Return, I beseech you, from your evil ways,
And from your evil doings ;
But they did not hear, they did not attend unto me,
Saith Jehovah.

5. Your fathers, where are they ?
And the prophets, do they live forever ?

6. But my words, and my statutes,
Which I commanded my servants, the prophets,
Have they not overtaken your fathers ?
And they returned and said ; (*after this,*)
Like as Jehovah of Hosts hath thought to do unto us,
According to our ways and according to our doings,
So hath he done unto us.'

Part II.—The Visions.

Chapter 1: 7—Chapter 6.

Vision I.   Ch. 1 : 7—17.—*The man among the myrtles.*

: 7.   On the twenty-fourth day of the eleventh month, which is the month of Sebat, (*February*,) in the second year of Darius, came the word of Jehovah to Zechariah, the son

8.   of Berechiah, the son of Iddo, the prophet, saying : I saw that night, and behold a man riding upon a red horse, and he stood among the myrtles in the valley, and behind him

9.   there were red, bay and white horses.   And I said, 'My lord, what are these ?'   And the angel that talked with

10.   me, said unto me, 'I will show thee what they are.'   And the man that stood among the myrtles answered and said, 'These are they whom Jehovah hath sent to walk

11.   throughout the earth.'   And they answered the angel of Jehovah that stood among the myrtles, 'We have walked throughout the earth, and behold all the earth dwells and

12.   is at rest.'   Then the angel of Jehovah answered and said, ' Oh Jehovah of Hosts!
How long wilt thou not pity Jerusalem
And the cities of Judah,
Against which thou hast been angry these seventy years ?'

13.   And Jehovah answered the angel that talked with me good words and consoling words.

14.   And the angel that talked with me said unto me, Cry, saying, 'Thus saith Jehovah of Hosts,
I am jealous for Jerusalem, and for Zion, with great jealousy.

15.   And I am inflamed with great anger against the secure nations,
For I was but a little angry, (*against Jerusalem and Zion*,)
But they aggravated the affliction.

16.   Therefore thus saith Jehovah,
I am returned to Jerusalem with mercies,
My house (*temple*) shall be built in it,
Saith Jehovah of Hosts.
And a (*measuring*) line shall be stretched forth upon Jerusalem.

17. Cry also, saying,
Thus saith Jehovah of Hosts,
My cities shall also be extended by prosperity,
And Jehovah shall yet comfort Zion,
And shall yet choose Jerusalem.'

VISION II.   Ch. 1: 18—21.—*The four horns and four artificers.*

18. And I lifted up mine eyes, and saw, and behold four horns.
19. And I said unto the angel that talked with me, 'What
are these?'   And he answered me, 'These are the horns
that have scattered Judah, Israel and Jerusalem.'
20, 21.   And Jehovah showed me four artificers.   And I said,
'What do these come to do?'   And he replied, saying,
'These are the horns that have scattered Judah, so that
a man could not lift up his head; but those are come to
terrify them, to cast out the horns of the nations which
lifted up the horn over the land of Judah to scatter it.'

VISION III.   Ch. 2.—*The man with the measuring line.*

2 : 1.   And I lifted up mine eyes, and looked and behold a man,
2.   and in his hand a measuring line.   And I said, 'Where
art thou going?'   And he said unto me, 'To measure Jerusalem, to see what is its breadth, and what is its length.
3.   And behold, the angel that talked with me went forth,
4.   and another angel came out to meet him, And said unto
him, Run, speak to this young man (*Zechariah*), saying,
Jerusalem shall inhabit villages,
For the multitude of men and cattle in her midst.
5.   And I will be to her, saith Jehovah,
A wall of fire around,
And for a glory will I be in her midst.
6.   Ho! Ho! fly then from the north country, saith Jehovah,
For as the four winds of heaven have I scattered you, saith
Jehovah.
7.   O Zion! deliver thyself,
Thou that dwellest with the daughter of Babylon.
8.   For thus saith Jehovah of Hosts:
After the glory hath he sent me
To the nations that spoiled you,

For he that toucheth you,
Toucheth the pupil of his own eye.

9. For, behold, I will shake my hand (*fist*) over them,
And they shall be a spoil to their own servants;
And ye shall acknowledge
That Jehovah of Hosts hath sent me.

10. Sing and rejoice, O daughter of Zion,
For behold I come;
And I will dwell in thy midst,
Saith Jehovah.

11. And many nations shall be joined to Jehovah in that day,
And shall be to me for a people,
And I will dwell in the midst of them,
And thou shalt know
That Jehovah of Hosts hath sent me unto thee.

12. And Jehovah shall inherit Judah,
His portion, in a land of holiness,
And shall choose again Jerusalem.

13. Be silent, all flesh, before Jehovah,
Because he is arisen from the habitation of his holiness.'

VISION IV. Ch. 3.—*Joshua the High Priest before the angel of* JEHOVAH.

3 : 1. And he showed me Joshua, the high priest, standing before
the angel of Jehovah, and Satan standing at his right

2. hand to accuse him. And Jehovah said to Satan,
' Jehovah rebuke thee O Satan!
Jehovah rebuke thee! he that chooses Jerusalem!
Is not this a brand plucked from the fire ?'

3. And Joshua was clothed in filthy garments and stood be-
4. fore the angel. And he answered and spake to those who
stood before him, saying, ' Take the filthy garments away
from him;' and he said to him (*Joshua*), ' Behold I take
away from thee thy sins, and they shall clothe thee with
5. festal garments.' Then I said, ' Let them place a clean
tiara upon his head;' and they placed a clean tiara upon
his head, and they put garments upon him, and the angel
6. of Jehovah was (*still*) standing (*there*). And the angel
of Jehovah answered to Joshua, saying,

7. ' Thus saith Jehovah of Hosts,
If thou wilt walk in my ways,

And if thou wilt keep my laws,
Thou shalt judge my house,
And also keep my courts,
And I will give thee guides among these that are standing
    here.

8. Hear, I beseech thee O Joshua, the high priest,
    Thou and thy colleagues who sit before thee,
    For men of omen are they;
    For behold I bring my servant, BRANCH.

9. For behold the stone which I have laid before Joshua,
    Upon this one stone shall there be seven eyes,
    Behold, carving I will carve it,
    Saith Jehovah of Hosts,
    And I will remove the sin of the land in one day.

10. In that day, saith Jehovah of Hosts,
    Ye shall call every man to his neighbor,
    Under the vine and under the fig-tree.'

VISION V. Ch. 4.—*The golden candlestick, and the two olive trees.*

4 : 1. And the angel who spoke with me returned, and awaked me
   2.   as a man who is awaked from his sleep; and he said un-
         to me, what seest thou ?   And I said, I have looked and
         behold a candlestick all of gold, and a bowl on the top of
         it, and its seven lamps upon it, and seven tubes to each
   3.   lamp on the top of it: and two olive trees, one on the right
   4.   hand of the bowl, and·one on the left hand.   And I an-
         swered and spake to the angel that talked with me, say-
         ing, 'What are these, my lord ?'
   5. Then the angel that talked with me answered and said unto
         me, 'Dost thou not know what these are ?' And I said, no,
         my lord.
   6. Then he answered and spake unto me, saying, This is the
         word of Jehovah unto Zerubbabel, saying,
      Not by might, and not by power,
      But by my spirit,
      Saith Jehovah of Hosts.
   7. Who art thou, thou great mountain before Zerubbabel ?
      Be a plain! He shall bring forth the top stone with shoutings,
      Grace! Grace unto it.

8. And the word of Jehovah came unto me saying,
9. The hands of Zerubbabel have founded this house,
    And his hands shall finish it,
    And thou shalt know
    That Jehovah of Hosts hath sent me unto you.
10. For who will despise the day of small things?
    For they shall rejoice and see
    The plummet in the hand of Zerubbabel,
    These seven eyes of Jehovah,
    They run to and fro in the whole earth.
11. And I answered and said unto him, What are these two
    olive trees on the right hand of the candlestick, and on
12. the left? And I answered again and said unto him,
    What are the two olive branches which through the tubes
13. of gold pour out the golden oil from themselves? And
    he answered unto me, saying, Knowest thou not what
14. these are? And I said, no, my lord. These are the two
    sons of oil, that stand by the Lord of the whole earth.

VISION VI. Ch. 5: 1—14.—*The flying roll.*

5 : 1. Then I turned and raised my eyes, and looked, and behold
   2.   a flying roll. And he (*the interpreting angel*) said unto me,
        'What dost thou see?' And I said, 'I see a flying roll,
   3.   in length twenty cubits, and in breadth ten cubits.' Then
        he said unto me,
        'This is the curse that goes forth before the face of the
        whole land,
        For every thief shall be cut off according to this side,
        And every perjurer shall be cut off according to that side.
   4.   I have caused it to go forth, saith Jehovah of Hosts,
        And it shall go into the house of the thief,
        And into the house of him that swears falsely by my name,
        And it shall dwell in the midst of it,
        And it consumes their house, and its wood and its stone.'

VISION VII. Ch. 5: 5—11.—*The woman in the Ephah.*

5. Then the angel that talked with me went forth, and said
    unto me, 'Lift up, I pray thee, thine eyes, and see

6. what this is that goeth forth.' And I said, 'What is this?' And he said, 'This is the ephah which goeth forth,' and he said, 'This is their appearance in all the
7. land.' And behold a talent of lead was lifted up. But this is a woman that is sitting in the midst of the ephah.
8. And he said, 'This is wickedness.' And he thrust her down into the midst of the ephah, and he cast the
9. stone of lead upon its mouth. And I raised my eyes and saw, and behold two women came out, and the wind in their wings, for they had wings like the wings of a stork, and they raised the ephah between earth and heaven.
10. And I said to the angel that talked with me, 'Where do
11. these carry the ephah?' And he said unto me, 'To build for it a house in the land of Shinar: and it (*the house*) shall be settled and fixed on its own base.'

VISION VIII. Ch. 6: 1—8.—*The four chariots.*

6 : 1. And I turned and lifted up mine eyes and saw, and behold four chariots came out from between two mountains, and
2. the mountains were mountains of brass. In the first
3. chariot were red horses; and in the second chariot black horses; and in the third chariot white horses; and the
4. fourth chariot piebald and fleet (*or strong*) horses. And I answered and said unto the angel that talked with me,
5. 'What are these, my lord?' And the angel answered and said unto me, 'These are the four winds of the heavens, going forth from standing before the Lord of the whole
6. earth. That which has the black horses goes forth to the north country, and the white go forth following them;
7. and the piebald go forth to the south country.' And the fleet went forth, and they desired to go that they might walk through the earth; and he said, 'Go walk through
8. the earth,' and they walked through the earth. And he cried to me, and spake to me saying, 'Behold these that go forth into the land of the north have quieted my spirit in the land of the north.'

VISION IX. Ch. 6 : 9—15.—*The crown on Joshua's head.*

9, 10. And the word of Jehovah came unto me saying : 'Take of (*them of*) the captivity of Heldai, of Tobijah, of Jedaiah, and go thou in that day, and go to the house of Josiah the son of Zephaniah, who (*all*) have come from Babylon:

11. and take thou silver and gold, and make crowns, and place them on the head of Joshua the son of Jozedek,

12. the high priest. And speak to him saying, Thus saith Jehovah of Hosts : Behold a man whose name is BRANCH, From his place shall he grow up, And he shall build the temple of Jehovah.

13. And he shall build the temple of Jehovah, And he shall bear majesty, And he sits and reigns upon his throne, And is a priest upon his throne, And the council of peace shall be between them both.'

14. And the crowns shall be to Helem and to Tobijah, and to Jedaiah, and to Hen the son of Zephaniah, for a memorial

15. in the temple of Jehovah. And the far-off shall come and build in the temple of Jehovah, and ye shall know that Jehovah of Hosts hath sent me unto you, and it shall be thus (*to you*) if ye will listen to the voice of Jehovah your God.

PART III.—DIDACTIC.

CHAPTERS 7, 8.

The Query.

7 : 1. And it was so in the fourth year of Darius the king, that the word of Jehovah was to Zechariah in the fourth (day)

2. of the ninth month, in Chisleu. And Bethel sent Shere-zer and Regem Melech, and their men, to pray before the

3. face of Jehovah ; and to speak to the priests which were in the house of Jehovah of Hosts, and to the prophets, saying : ' Ought I to weep in the fifth month, separating myself, as I have done for so many years ?'

The Reproof.

4. Then was the word of Jehovah of Hosts to me, saying :
5. 'Speak unto all the people of the land, and to the priests, saying, When ye fasted and mourned in the fifth and seventh month, these seventy years, did ye fast unto me?
6. unto me ? And when ye ate, and when ye drank, was it not to yourselves that ye were eating, and to yourselves that ye were drinking ?'
7. Are not these the words which Jehovah cried by the hand of the former prophets, when Jerusalem was inhabited and in peace, and also her cities round about her, and when the south and the plain was inhabited.'
8. And the word of Jehovah was to Zechariah saying :
9. 'Thus spake Jehovah of Hosts saying :
Judge the judgment of truth,
And work kindness and compassion,
Every man toward his neighbor :
10. And the widow, and the fatherless,
The stranger and the poor, do not oppress,
And do not devise evil in your hearts,
Any man against his neighbor.
11. But they (*your fathers*) refused to hear,
And presented a refractory shoulder (*one that refused to wear the yoke*),
And made heavy their ears against hearing :
12. And their heart they made an adamant
Against hearing the law,
And the words which Jehovah of Hosts did send in his spirit
By the hand of the former prophets,
Wherefore there was great wrath from Jehovah of Hosts.
13. And it came to pass,
That as He cried and they did not hear,
So they cry and I hear not,
Saith Jehovah of Hosts.
14. And I scattered them to all nations whom they knew not,
And the land was desolate after them,
So that none went out or came in,
And they made the land of desire to be desolate.'

Promises.

8 : 1. 'And the word of Jehovah of Hosts was to me saying.

2. Thus saith Jehovah of Hosts,
I was jealous toward Zion with great jealousy,
And with great fury was I jealous toward her.

3. Thus saith Jehovah, I have returned to Zion,
And I will dwell in the midst of Jerusalem,
And Jerusalem shall be called " city of the truth,"
And the mountain of Jehovah, " mountain of holiness." '

4. 'Thus saith Jehovah of Hosts,
There shall yet sit old men and old women,
In the streets of Jerusalem,
And the man whose staff is in his hand for multitude of
days.

5. And the streets of the city shall be full of boys and girls,
Playing in the streets of it.'

6. 'Thus saith Jehovah of Hosts,
If it is wonderful in the eyes of the remnant of this people
in these days,
Is it also wonderful in my eyes,
Saith Jehovah of Hosts ?'

7. 'Thus saith Jehovah of Hosts,
Behold, I am he saving my people,
From the land of the east, and from the land of the setting
sun.

8. And I will lead them, (viz. *from these lands to Jerusalem,*)
And they shall dwell in the midst of Jerusalem,
And they shall be my people,
And I will be their God, in truth and righteousness.'

9. 'Thus saith Jehovah of Hosts,
Strengthen your hands, ye that in these days hear these
words
By the mouth of the (*same*) prophets who (*were*) in that day,
When the house of Jehovah of Hosts was founded,
That the temple might be built.

10. For before these days there was no hire of a man,
And hire of a beast, there was also none.
And to him going out and coming in, (*the traveller,*)
There was no peace from the enemy,
And I stirred up all men, every man against his neighbor.

11. But now, not as in the former days, (*will*) I (*be*)
    To the remnant of this people,
    Saith Jehovah of Hosts.
12. For the seed shall be safe, (*Heb. of peace,*)
    The vine shall give her fruit,
    And the earth shall give her produce,
    And the heavens shall give their dew,
    And I will cause the remnant of this people
    To inherit all these things.
13. And it shall be, that as ye have been a curse among the
       nations,
    Oh house of Judah, and house of Israel,
    So I will save you, and ye shall be a blessing :
    Fear not, (*therefore,*) strengthen your hands.'
14. ' For thus saith Jehovah of Hosts,
    As I determined to punish you (*the house of Israel*)
    When your fathers provoked me,
    Saith Jehovah of Hosts,
    And I repented not,
15. So, on the contrary, I have determined, in these days,
    To do good to Jerusalem, and to the house of Judah,
    Fear not.
16. These are the words which ye must do, (*obey,*)
    Speak the truth, every man to his neighbor ;
    Truth and the judgment of peace judge in your gates ;
17. Devise not evil in your hearts,
    Each man against his neighbor,
    And an oath of falsehood do not love,
    For all these are the things which I hate,
    Saith Jehovah.'

The Reply.

18. And the word of Jehovah of Hosts was to me, saying,
19. Thus saith Jehovah of Hosts,
    ' The fast of the fourth (*month*), and the fast of the fifth,
    And the fast of the seventh, and the fast of the tenth,
    Shall be to the house of Judah for joy and gladness,
    And for festal observances,
    Therefore love the truth and peace.'

Promises to the Church.

20. Thus saith Jehovah of hosts,
    ' It shall yet be that peoples shall come,
    And the inhabitants of many cities.
21. And they shall go, the inhabitants of one (*city*) to another,
    Saying, ' Let us go to pray before Jehovah
    And to seek Jehovah of Hosts.'
    ' I will go also.'
22. And they shall come, many peoples and many nations,
    To seek Jehovah of Hosts in Jerusalem,
    And to pray before Jehovah.
23. Thus saith Jehovah of Hosts,
    In those days (*it shall be*) that they shall seize (*viz.:*)
    Ten men from all the tongues of the nations,
    They shall seize the skirt of a man (*that is*) a Jew,
    Saying, ' We will go with you,
    For we have heard that God is with you.'

Part IV.—Prophetic.

Chapters 9—14.

I. *The Syrian Conquests of Alexander.*

Ch. 9 : 1—8.

1. *A Burden.*
   The word of Jehovah on the land of Hadrach,
   And Damascus shall be its rest,
   For to Jehovah is the sight of man,
   And all the tribes of Israel.
2. Also Hamath shall border on it,
   Tyre and Sidon because it is very wise.
3. And Tyre has built for herself a strong hold,
   And has heaped up silver as dust,
   And gold as the mire of the streets.
4. Behold the Lord will dispossess her,
   And will cast into the sea her bulwark,
   And she shall be consumed with fire.

7

5. Ashkelon shall see it and fear,
   Gaza (*shall see it*) and tremble greatly,
   And Ekron, for her reliance is disgraced,
   And a King shall perish from Gaza,
   And Ashkelon shall not be inhabited.
6. An alien shall dwell in Ashdod,
   And I will destroy the pride of the Philistines.
7. And I will remove his blood from his mouth,
   And his abominations from between his teeth,
   And he that remains, even he, shall be for our God,
   And he shall be as a prince in Judah,
   And Ekron as the Jebusite.
8. And I will encamp around my house because of the army,
   Because of the passer by, and because of the returner,
   And the exactor shall no more pass through them,
   For now I see with mine eyes.

II. *The lowly King Messiah.*

Ch. 9 : 9, 10.

9. Rejoice greatly, daughter of Zion,
   Shout for joy, daughter of Jerusalem,
   Behold ! thy King cometh unto thee,
   Just, and endowed with salvation, is he,
   Lowly and riding upon an ass,
   And upon a foal, the son of she-asses.
10. And I will cut off the chariot from Ephraim,
    And the horse from Jerusalem,
    And the bow of war shall be cut off,
    And he shall speak peace to the nations,
    And his dominion (*be*) from sea to sea,
    And from the river to the ends of the earth.

III. *The Maccabean Deliverance.*

Ch. 9 : 11—17.

11. Also thou—in the blood of thy covenant
    I have sent forth thy prisoners,
    From the pit, and there is no water in it.

12. Return to the strong hold, O prisoners of hope !
    Even to-day (*am I*) declaring, I will render double to you.
13. For I have bent to me Judah,
    The bow have I filled with Ephraim,
    And I have raised up thy sons, O Zion !
    Against thy sons, O Javan !
    And have made thee as the sword of a mighty man.
14. And over them Jehovah will appear,
    And his arrow goes forth like lightning,
    And the Lord Jehovah shall blow the trumpet,
    And he goes forth in the storms of the south.
15. Jehovah of hosts will protect them,
    And they eat, and they trample under foot the sling-stones,
    And they drink, and make a noise as from wine,
    And they are full as the altar-bowls,
    And as the corners of the altar.
16. And Jehovah their God will save them in that day,
    As a flock (*will he save*) his people,
    For as gems of a diadem are they lifted up in his land.
17. For how great is his goodness !
    And how great his beauty !
    Corn makes the young men to grow,
    And new wine the maidens.

IV. *Prayer and Promise.*

Ch. 10 : 1—5.

1. Ask of Jehovah rain,
    In the time of the latter rain ;
    Jehovah shall (*then*) cause lightnings,
    And shall give abundant rain,
    To every man grass in his field.
2. For the teraphim speak nothingness ;
    And the soothsayers see falsehood ;
    And the dreams speak vanity ;
    They comfort falsely ;
    Wherefore they wander as a flock,
    They are troubled because there is no shepherd.
3. Against the shepherds my anger is kindled,
    And the he-goats will I punish,

For Jehovah of Hosts visits his flock, the house of Judah,
And makes them like a caparisoned horse in war,

4. From him (*is*) the corner-stone, and from him the pin,
From him the bow of battle,
From him comes forth every ruler together.

5. And they shall be as heroes,
Trampling on the mire of the streets in war,
And they fight, for Jehovah is with them,
And the riders on horses are put to shame.

V. *The Restoration of the Jews.*

Ch. 10 : 6—12.

6. And I will strengthen the house of Judah,
And I will save the house of Joseph,
And I will again cause them to dwell,
For I have compassion upon them ;
And they shall be as though I had not cast them out,
For I am Jehovah their God, and I will hear them.

7. And Ephraim shall be as a mighty man,
Their heart shall rejoice as (*with*) wine,
And their sons shall see and rejoice,
Their heart shall rejoice in Jehovah.

8. I will hiss to them and collect them,
For I have redeemed them,
And they shall be many as they were before.

9. And I will sow them among the peoples,
And in distant lands they shall remember me,
And with their children they shall live and return.

10. And I will bring them back from the land of Egypt,
And from Assyria will I gather them,
And to the land of Gilead and Lebanon will I bring them,
And there shall not be room to contain them.

11. And he passes through the sea, the affliction,
And he smites in the sea the waves,
And all the deeps of the river are put to shame,
And the pride of Assyria is overthrown,
And the rod of Egypt shall give way.

12. And I will strengthen them in Jehovah,
    And in his name shall they walk,
    Saith Jehovah.

VI.   *The Mission of Messiah.*

CHAP. 11.

(1.) *The storm preceding the coming of Christ.*

Ch. 11 : 1—3.

1. Open, O Lebanon, thy gates,
   And let the fire consume thy cedars.
2. Howl, O cypress, for the cedar falls,
   For the lofty are laid waste,
   Howl, O ye oaks of Bashan,
   For the thick forest falls.
3. A voice of howling of the shepherds !
   For their glory is laid waste :
   A voice of roaring of the lions !
   For the pride of Jordan is laid waste.

(2.) *Christ assuming the pastoral care of the Theocratic people.*

V. 4—14.

4. Thus saith Jehovah my God,
   'Feed the flock of slaughter.
5. Whose buyers slaughter them,
   And do not become guilty :
   And whose sellers say,
   Blessed be Jehovah, for I am enriched,
   And their shepherds spare them not.
6. For I will no longer spare the dwellers in this land,
   Saith Jehovah,
   And behold ! I will give up each man
   To the hand of his neighbor,
   And to the hand of his king,
   And they lay waste the land,
   And I will not deliver out of their hand.'
7. So I fed the flock of slaughter,
   In order that (*I might preserve*) the humble of the flock,

And I took to myself two staves,
The one I called Favor,
The other I called Union,
And I fed the flock.

8. And I destroyed three shepherds in one month,
And my soul was grieved with them,
And their soul abhorred me.

9. Then I said, I will not feed you,
The dying, let them die,
The cut off, let them be cut off,
The remaining, let them consume each the flesh of the other.

10. And I took my staff Favor and brake it ;
To abolish my covenant that I had made with all nations.

11. And it (*the covenant*) was abolished in that day,
And thus they knew (*viz.*)
The humble of the flock who clung to me,
That this is the word of Jehovah.

12. Then I said to them,
If it seem good in your eyes, give me my reward,
And if not, withhold it.
And they weighed my reward, thirty pieces of silver !

13. And Jehovah said to me,
Cast it to the potter,
This magnificent price at which I was valued of them,
And I took the thirty pieces of silver,
And I cast it down in the house of Jehovah,
(*To be given thence*) to the potter.

14. And I broke my second staff Union,
To destroy the brotherhood between Judah and Israel.

(3.) *The curse of evil rulers after the rejection of Christ.*

Ch. 11 : 15—17.

15. And Jehovah said to me,
' Again, take to thee the implements of a foolish shepherd.

16. For behold ! I raise up a shepherd in the land.
The perishing will he not visit,
The straying will he not seek out,
The wounded will he not heal,
The feeble will he not nourish,

And the flesh of the fat ones will he eat
And their hoofs will he break off.
17. Wo to the worthless shepherd, forsaking the flock !
A sword upon his arm !
And upon his right eye !
His arm shall surely be withered,
And his right eye shall surely be blind.'

VII.   *Future blessings to Judah.*

Ch. 12 : 1—9.

1. *A Burden.*
   ' The word of Jehovah upon Israel,
   Saith Jehovah, who stretches the Heavens,
   And establishes the earth,
   And forms the spirit of man within him.
2. Behold ! I make Jerusalem a threshold of shaking
   To all nations round about,
   And also upon Judah shall it be,
   In the siege against Jerusalem.
3. And it shall be in that day,
   I will make Jerusalem a stone of burden to all the nations.
   All who lift it up shall surely gash themselves,
   And there shall be gathered against her all people of the
     earth.
4. In that day, saith Jehovah,
   I will smite every horse with affright,
   And his rider with madness,
   And upon the house of Judah will I open my eyes,
   And every horse of the nations will I smite with blindness.
5. And the princes of Judah say in their hearts,
   My strength (*is*) the inhabitants of Jerusalem,
   In Jehovah of Hosts, their God.
6. In that day I will make the princes of Judah
   As a pan of fire among faggots,
   And as a torch of fire in a sheaf,
   And they shall consume on the right hand and on the left
   All the nations round about,
   And Jerusalem shall yet sit in her own place in Jerusa-
     lem.

7. And Jehovah shall help the tents of Judah first,
    That the glory of the house of David,
    And the glory of the inhabitant of Jerusalem,
    May not be magnified over Judah.
8. In that day Jehovah will protect the dweller in Jerusalem,
    And the feeble among them in that day shall be as David,
    And the house of David as God,
    As the angel of Jehovah before them.
9. And it shall be in that day
    I will seek to destroy all nations
    Who come up against Jerusalem.'

VIII. *Future repentance and blessing to Jerusalem.*

Ch. 12 : 10—14.

10. And I pour out upon the house of David,
     And upon the inhabitants of Jerusalem,
     A spirit of grace and of supplication,
     And they look upon me, whom they pierced,
     And they lament for him, as the lamenting of an only child,
     And they mourn for him, as the mourning of a first-born.
11. And in that day the mourning shall be great in Jerusalem,
     As the mourning of Hadadrimmon in the vale of Megiddo.
12. And the land mourns, family by family apart,
     The family of the house of David apart and their wives
          apart,
     The family of the house of Nathan apart and their wives
          apart,
13. The family of the house of Levi apart and their wives apart,
     The family of the house of Shimei apart and their wives
          apart,
14. All the remaining families,
     Family by family apart, and their wives apart.

IX. *Fruits of penitence.*

Ch. 13 : 1—6.

1. In that day there shall be a fountain opened,
    To the house of David, and to the inhabitants of Jerusalem,
    For sin, and for uncleanness.

c

2. And it shall be in that day, saith Jehovah of Hosts,
    I will cut off the names of the idols from the land,
    And they shall not be remembered any more ;
    And also the prophets, and the spirit of uncleanness
    Will I remove from the land.
3. And it happens, if a man still prophesy,
    His father and his mother who begat him say unto him,
    ' Thou shalt not live,
    Because thou hast spoken falsehood in the name of Jehovah,'
    And his father and his mother who begat him,
    Pierce him through in his prophesying.
4. And it happens in that day, the prophets are ashamed
    From their vision in their prophesying,
    And they shall no longer put on the mantle of hair to deceive.
5. And he says, ' I am not a prophet, I am a husbandman,
    For a man has sold me from the time of my youth.'
6. And he (*the former*) says unto him,
    ' What then are these wounds between thy hands ?'
    And he replies : ' (*they are the wounds*)
    Which I received in the house of my lovers.'

X.   *The sword awaking against the shepherd.*

Ch. 13 : 7—9.

7. O sword ! awake against my shepherd,
    Against a man, my nearest kin,
    Saith Jehovah of Hosts.
    Smite the shepherd,
    And the sheep shall be scattered,
    And I will bring back my hand upon the little ones.
8. And it shall be in all the land, saith Jehovah,
    Two portions shall be cut off and die,
    And the third portion shall remain in it.
9. And I bring the third part into the fire
    And purify them as silver is purified,
    And try them as gold is tried.
    They shall call upon my name,
    And I will hear them,
    I will say they are my people,
    And they shall say, Jehovah is my God.

XI. *Future glories of the Church.*

CHAP. 14.

1. Behold a day comes to Jehovah.
   And thy spoil is divided in the midst of thee.
2. And I collect all the nations against Jerusalem to battle,
   And the city is taken, and the houses plundered,
   And the women dishonored,
   And half the city go forth into captivity,
   And the remnant of the city shall not be cut off from the
   city.
3. And Jehovah goes forth and fights against those heathen,
   As in the day of his conflict, in the day of battle.
4. And his feet shall stand in that day on the mount of Olives,
   Which is before Jerusalem on the east,
   And the mount of Olives is split in the midst
   From east to west, a great valley
   And half the mountain recedes to the north, and half to the
   south.
5. And ye flee into my mountain valley,
   For the mountain valley will extend to Azal,
   And ye shall flee, as ye fled before the earthquake,
   In the days of Uzziah, king of Judah,
   And there comes Jehovah my God, all holy ones with thee.
6. And it shall be in that day,
   It shall not be light, precious things are obscured.
7. And it shall be one day, it shall be known to Jehovah,
   Not day, and not night,
   And it shall be that in the evening time it shall be light.
8. And it shall be in that day,
   Living waters shall go out from Jerusalem,
   Their half to the eastern sea,
   And their half to the western sea,
   In summer and winter it shall be.
9. And Jehovah shall be king over the whole land,
   In that day Jehovah shall be one, and his name one.
10. All the land shall be changed,
    As the plain from Geba to Rimmon, south of Jerusalem,
    And she shall be exalted and sit in her place,

From the gate of Benjamin to the place of the first gate,
To the gate of the corner,
And from the tower of Hananeel to the king's wine presses.

11. And they dwell in her,
And there shall be no more curse,
And Jerusalem sits in security.

12. And this shall be the plague, with which Jehovah shall
plague
All nations which warred against Jerusalem,
His flesh shall rot, and he standing on his feet,
And his eyes shall rot in their sockets,
And their tongue shall rot in their mouth.

13. And it shall be in that day,
There shall be among them a great confusion from Jehovah,
And they shall seize each man the hand of his neighbor,
And his hand shall rise against the hand of his neighbor.

14. And Judah also shall fight in Jerusalem,
And the wealth of all the nations round about shall be gath-
ered ;
Gold, and silver, and garments in great abundance.

15. And so shall be the plague of the horse, the mule, the camel,
and the ass,
Which shall be in these camps, as this plague.

16. And it shall be that the remnant of all the nations,
Who came up against Jerusalem,
Shall go up from year to year, (*to Jerusalem*,)
To worship the king, Jehovah of Hosts,
And to keep the feast of tabernacles.

17. And it shall be that whoever of the tribes of the earth,
Will not go up to Jerusalem to worship the king, Jehovah
of Hosts,
Upon them there shall be no rain.

18. And if the family of Egypt will not go forth, and come up,
And there shall not be upon them (*therefore any rain*,)
There shall be the plague with which Jehovah shall plague
the nations,
That do not come up to keep the feast of tabernacles.

19. And this will be the sin of Egypt and the sin of all nations,
That come not up to keep the feast of tabernacles.

20. In that day there shall be upon the bells of the horses
" SACRED TO JEHOVAH."
And the vessels in the house of Jehovah shall be,
As the sacrificial bowls upon the altar.

21. And every vessel in Jerusalem and Judah shall be,
SACRED TO JEHOVAH OF HOSTS.
And all the sacrificers shall come, and take from them and
offer in them,
And there shall be no more a Canaanite
In the house of Jehovah of Hosts, in that day.

INTRODUCTION TO ZECHARIAH.

THE name Zechariah (*remembrance of Jehovah*, or *one whom Jehovah remembers*) was common among the Jews, as appears from the fact that four others besides the prophet are mentioned in the Old Testament. Like Jeremiah and Ezekiel, he was a priest as well as a prophet. In the prophecy he is called the son of Barachiah, the son of Iddo ; whilst in Ezra 5 : 1, 6 : 14, he is simply called the son of Iddo. From this fact it has been inferred that he was not the grandson of Iddo, but his son, and that Iddo and Barachiah are names for the same person. But the fact probably is, that his father died when he was very young, and therefore in the priestly genealogy he was reckoned as the son of his grandfather, a reckoning which the flexibility of all terms of relationship among the Jews made not uncommon.

Of his personal history we know but little, except that he entered early on the discharge of his prophetic duties, (ch. 2 : 4.) Some have supposed that our Lord referred to him in Matt. 23 : 35, when he speaks of Zechariah, the son of Barachiah, who perished between the porch and the altar. But there is no evidence whatever that this prophet thus died. There is a Zechariah, who died in this way, mentioned in 2 Chron. 24 : 21, to whom it is much more probable that the allusion is made. He was, it is true, the son of Jehoiada, but, aside from the fact that double names are mentioned in the same way elsewhere, as in the case of Hobab, the more familiar name Barachiah might readily creep into the text from the margin to take the place of the less familiar Jehoiada, or to define the name Zechariah, that was perhaps left without any patronymic. The reason for referring to him is found in the arrangement of the Hebrew Old Testament, by which 2 Chronicles is the last book in the volume, thus making Zechariah the last martyr of whom they would read, as Abel was the first.

His family seems to have returned from Babylon with the first expedition in the reign of Cyrus, and as this was eighteen years before the date of the prophecy, in which he is expressly called a young man, he must have been very young at the time of his return. He had seen the arresting of the erection of the temple by the successful machinations of the Samaritans in the Persian Court, and the depressed tone of the national character during the time that followed this arrest. He had witnessed the growth of that selfish greed for their own individual interests, and their neglect of the interests of religion, that was so mournful a characteristic of this period. He had also seen the creeping feebleness with which the work of rebuilding the temple was undertaken and prosecuted, when the edict of permission was again issued, by Darius Hystaspis. Now, as the temple was to them the grand symbol of revealed religion, indifference to it was an undoubted symptom of backsliding and spiritual declension. It was therefore necessary that they should be stirred up to the discharge of their duty as to the temple, and awakened to a proper estimate of that great plan of mercy to the world, of which the temple and the theocracy were but symbols, in order that their zeal might have at once a right motive and a right direction. Hence Haggai was first raised up to rouse them to activity in building the temple, and two months later Zechariah followed to take up the same theme and unfold it yet more richly to the minds of the people, by connecting the poor and passing present, with the magnificent and enduring future. The scope of the prophecy then is to produce a genuine revival of religion among the people, and thus encourage them in the right way to engage in the rebuilding of the temple.

The date of the prophecy is recorded very accurately, and is identical with that of Haggai, the second year of Darius Hystaspis, B. C. 520.

In regard to the literary characteristics of the prophecy, Henderson remarks :—"In point of style, our prophet varies, according to the nature of his subjects, and the manner in which they were presented to his mind. He now expresses himself in simple, conversational prose, now in poetry. At one time he abounds in the language of symbols; at another, in that of direct prophetical announcement. His symbols are, for the most part, enigmatical, and require the explanations which accompany them. His prose resembles most that of Ezekiel; it is diffuse, uniform, and repetitious. His prophetic poetry possesses much of the elevation and dignity to be found in the earlier prophets, with whose writings he appears to have been familiar; only his rhythmus is sometimes harsh and unequal, while his parallelisms are destitute of that symmetry and finish which form some of the principal beauties of Hebrew poetry."

The prophecy consists of four parts : I. *Introductory*, ch. 1 : 1—6; II. *Symbolical*, ch. 1 : 7 to the end of ch. 6, containing nine visions; III. *Didactic*, chs. 7 and 8; and, IV. *Prophetic*, ch. 9 to the end.

———

PART I.—INTRODUCTORY.—CH. 1 : 1—6.

ANALYSIS.

I. The warning from the example of their fathers, who were disobedient to the word of the Lord, and therefore punished, (v. 1, 2.)

II. The exhortation to avoid their sins, (v. 3, 4.)

III. The fate of their fathers pressed as a reason for listening to his message, which he was then about to deliver, (v. 5, 6.)

COMMENTARY.

CHAPTER I.

1 In the eighth month, in the second year of Darius, came the word of the Lord unto Zechariah, the son of Barachiah, the son of Iddo the prophet, saying,

2 The Lord hath been sore displeased with your fathers.

3 Therefore, say thou unto them, Thus saith the Lord of hosts, Turn ye unto me, saith the Lord of hosts,

1 : 1—6.—"In the eighth month, in the second year of Darius, came the word of Jehovah unto Zechariah, son of Barachiah, son of Iddo, the prophet, saying, Angry hath Jehovah been toward your fathers with (*great*) anger. Therefore say thou unto them, thus saith Jehovah of hosts, Return ye unto me, saith Jehovah of hosts, and I will return unto you, saith Jehovah of hosts. Be ye not as your fathers, unto whom the former prophets cried, saying : Thus saith Jehovah of hosts ; return, I beseech you, from your evil ways, and from your evil doings ; but they did not hear, they did not attend unto me, saith Jehovah. Your fathers, where are they ? And the prophets, do they live forever ? But my words, and my statutes, which I commanded my servants, the prophets, have they not overtaken your fathers ? And they returned and said ; (*after this,*) like as Jehovah of hosts hath thought to do unto us, according to our ways, and according to our doings, so hath he done unto us."

THE general meaning of this exordium is, God fulfilled all his threatenings to your fathers ; therefore beware, lest, by disobeying my voice, as they did that of

and I will turn unto you, saith the
LORD of hosts.

4 Be ye not as your fathers, unto whom the former prophets have cried, saying, Thus saith the LORD of hosts; Turn ye now from your evil ways, and

the earlier prophets, you suffer as did your fathers. It was, therefore, a most suitable introduction to the discharge of his prophetic functions.

The reference of the prophet is to the threatening of conquest and captivity to their fathers, and to the fulfilment of that threatening that was then before their eyes. And how complete was that fulfilment! The land that once flowed with milk and honey was now lying in widowed desolation and barrenness. The hills on whose green terraces once hung the climbing vine and the generous olive, were now bare and rugged. The cities and villages once echoing to the busy hum of a happy people, were now in ruins, and all over their once beautiful land had God written Ichabod. Thus far the meaning is plain.

The only difficulty is in the logical coherence of v. 5, with what precedes it. It seems to place the fathers who sinned and the prophets who obeyed on the same footing, as sharing the same fate. Hence some have suppose the reference was to false prophets, a supposition that completely dislocates the whole passage and overlooks the current of thought.

The object of the exordium is to show the unchanging permanence of God's word, by contrasting it with the transitory nature of their fathers and the prophets, and it may thus be set forth more fully.

from your evil doings ; but they did not
hear, nor hearken unto me, saith the
Lord.

5 Your fathers, where *are* they ? and
the prophets, do they live for ever ?
6 But my words and my statutes,

Let the fate of your fathers be a warning to you that
you avoid the disobedience to the word of Jehovah, which
brought upon them evils so desolating.   For where are
they now ?   Once they ruled and worshipped here as do
you.   The song of the Levite rang through the arches
of the temple, the smoke of the victim ascended from
its altars, their banners waved over these hills, and
their armies struck terror into the hearts of their enemies.   But where are they now ?   Some lie in slaughtered heaps, when the banner of Judah was trampled
in the dust, and her bravest sons cut down like grass
before the mower's scythe, by the fierce cohorts of the
Assyrian.   Some lie buried in the ruins of the holy city,
which they sought to defend from the spoiler.   Some
are sleeping by the flashing waters of the Euphrates, far
from the graves of their fathers, after weeping out a
weary life beneath the willows that bend in the land of
the stranger.   Whilst some in the feebleness of totter-
ing age have returned to lay their bones in the soil that
is hallowed by the memories and hopes of Israel.

And why has this been their mournful history ?   Because they refused to listen to the warnings of the
prophets.   Hence even the prophets themselves were
taken away.   They warned, and wept, and prayed, but
met only with stoning, reviling and hate.   They toiled
on to stay the coming judgments, but when their efforts
were disregarded by the people, God in mercy took

which I commanded my servants the prophets, did they not take hold of your fathers; and they returned and said, Like as the LORD of hosts thought to do unto us, according to our ways, and according to our doings, so hath he dealt with us.

them away from the evil to come. Then the last barrier was removed and the torrent of wrath came dire and pitiless in its rush of fury, and swept them away in its flood. Now as your fathers and the prophets alike have passed away, according to my word ; as neither the wickedness of the one, nor the piety of the other, could arrest my threatened judgments, beware lest a like evil come upon you, that your prophets being disregarded, be also withdrawn, and the judgments you are daring come upon you for your disobedience.

This appropriate introduction was probably followed with exhortations to build the temple and restore the worship of God, that are not recorded, as their interest was local and temporary, for its date is three months anterior to the next portion of the prophecy, and we cannot suppose all that time to have elapsed without any prophetic teachings of the people. That there were such instructions, and that they were obeyed by the people, would seem probable from the consolatory character of the next divine utterance that is recorded by the prophet in these visions.

PRACTICAL INFERENCES.

(1.) Whilst God is love, and whilst the preachers of the gospel must preach this glorious truth, they must not conceal the fact that God is a consuming fire, and angry with the wicked every day. It is a sign of a

7 ¶ Upon the four and twentieth day of the eleventh month, which *is* the month Sebat, in the second year of Darius, came the word of the Lord unto Zechariah, the son of Barachiah, the son of Iddo the prophet, saying,

8 I saw by night, and behold a man riding upon a red horse, and he stood

sickly piety when men are willing to hear nothing of the wrath of God against sin, (v. 1, 2.)

(2.) If men expect God to return to them in prosperity, they must return to him in penitence. The flower averted from the sun must turn toward it, to catch its genial smile, (v. 3.)

(3.) What we have to do for God in life should be done quickly, for life is rapidly passing ; to evil and good there comes alike the swift shadows of the sunset, (v. 5.)

(4.) What a man sows he shall also reap, and the seedings of life on earth shall be harvested in heaven or in hell, (v. 6.)

Part II.—The Visions.

Ch. 1 : 7 to end of Ch. 6.

Vision I.—Chapter 1: 7—17.

The Man among the Myrtles.

ANALYSIS.

I. The vision of a rider among the myrtles, surrounded with other riders, who bring him reports of the state of the earth, (v. 7—13.)

II. Explanation of this vision to the comfort of the Jewish people, and their encouragement in the work of rebuilding the city and temple, (v. 14—17.)

V. 7—17. " On the twenty-fourth day of the eleventh month, which is the month of Sebat (*February*), in the second year of Darius, came the word of JEHOVAH to Zechariah, the son of Berechiah, the son of Iddo, the prophet, saying : I saw

among the myrtle trees that *were* in the bottom ; and behind him *were there* red horses, speckled and white.

9 Then said I, O my lord, what *are* these ? And the angel that talked with me said unto me, I will show thee what these *be*.

that night, and behold a man riding upon a red horse, and he stood among the myrtles in the valley, and behind him there were red, bay and white horses. And I said, ' My lord, what are these ?' And the angel that talked with me, said unto me, ' I will show thee what they are.' And the man that stood among the myrtles answered and said, ' These are they whom Jehovah hath sent to walk throughout the earth.' And they answered the angel of Jehovah that stood among the myrtles, ' We have walked throughout the earth, and behold all the earth dwells and is at rest.' Then the angel of Jehovah answered and said, ' Oh Jehovah of Hosts ! how long wilt thou not pity Jerusalem and the cities of Judah, against which thou hast been angry these seventy years ?' And Jehovah answered the angel that talked with me good words and consoling words. And the angel that talked with me said unto me, Cry, saying, Thus saith Jehovah of Hosts, I am jealous for Jerusalem, and for Zion, with great jealousy. And I am inflamed with great anger against the secure nations. For I was but a little angry, (*against Jerusalem and Zion*,) but they aggravated the affliction. Therefore thus saith Jehovah, I am returned to Jerusalem with mercies, my house (*temple*) shall be built in it, saith Jehovah of Hosts, and a (*measuring*) line shall be stretched forth upon Jerusalem. Cry also, saying, thus saith Jehovah of Hosts, My cities shall also be extended by prosperity, and Jehovah shall yet comfort Zion, and shall yet choose Jerusalem."

THE object of this vision, or waking trance, is to comfort the disheartened people in their labor, by showing them the fact that God was with them, although they were very lowly and despised. This is done by exhibiting a symbolical picture of the theocratic people, which is explained to the prophet by an interpreting angel, who is not to be confounded with the angel of Jehovah, the central figure of the group.

10 And the man that stood among the myrtle trees answered and said, These *are they* whom the LORD hath sent to walk to and fro through the earth.

11 And they answered the angel of the LORD that stood among the myrtle trees, and said, We have walked to and fro through the earth, and, behold, all the earth sitteth still, and is at rest.

He sees a grove of myrtles, a beautiful shrub, with glossy, dark green leaves, and white, star-like clusters of fragrant flowers, whose leaves exhaled their richest odor only when bruised. This was a symbol of the theocracy, the Jewish Church and nation. The Church is not a cedar, in its queenly pride, or an oak in its giant strength, but a lowly myrtle, humble, unpretending, and exhaling its sweetest graces when bruised by the weight of affliction. Such was the existing state of the theocracy, and hence the despondency of the people, who thought that so lowly a thing must be wholly over-shadowed and destroyed by the proud and godless powers of the world.

But in the midst of these myrtles he sees a man on a red horse, whom we afterwards discover to be the angel of Jehovah, that divine person whom we trace all along the history of the Old Testament, in every manifestation of God to man, in visible form, until in the New Testament we find him manifest in the flesh. It is the second person of the mysterious Trinity, the great Head of the Church. The fact is thus symbolized that he is in the midst of the Church, unseen, and hence though seemingly so feeble and lowly, she has this inhabitation as her glory and defence. The celerity and strength of every agency connected with the Church, is set forth by

12 ¶ Then the angel of the LORD an-swered and said, O LORD of hosts, how long wilt thou not have mercy on Je-rusalem and on the cities of Judah, against which thou hast had indignation these threescore and ten years?

the horses, the red color of which signified the fervor of at once the zeal and the wrath of these agencies, as at once sanguine and sanguinary ; the white color, their triumphant strength, being the symbol of victory, and the bay, a combination of the two colors, showing the connection between these things in the arrangements made by God for the good of his Church. The sur-rounding angels on horses set forth the fact that God has provided every species of agency for the supply and defence of his Church, making the very powers of the world work to the promotion of her interests.

The attendant angels are sent to spy out the condi-tion of the whole earth, and bring back the report (v. 11) that all nations were in peace and prosperity. But Judea was lying in desolation, Jerusalem in ruins, and the temple but partially rebuilt. Here was a state of facts that seemed to contradict the promises of God to his people, and the threatenings of God to his enemies, and hence that tended to depress the one with doubt and inflate the other with pride. It was then time for God to work, and hence the divine angel begins (v. 12) to intercede for his people. Here, then, was an addi-tional fact of great comfort. Not only does Christ dwell in the midst of his people, and watch over all that affects their condition, but he intercedes for them, and his intercession is never in vain. This appears from v. 13, where in answer to these intercessions God speaks

13 And the LORD answered the angel that talked with me *with* good words *and* comfortable words.

14 So the angel that communed with me said unto me, Cry thou, saying, Thus saith the LORD of hosts ; 1 am jealous for Jerusalem and for Zion with a great jealousy.

comforting words to the angel, who was commissioned to speak to the prophet. These words are there recorded by the prophet in verses 14—17, and constitute the poetic exposition of the vision, in effect as follows :

Jerusalem and Zion are laid waste it is true, but not in anger, so much as in chastising love. God still loves them, and is jealous of any estrangement of their affections from him, and when estranged he chastises them to bring them back. This was his object in using the heathen as instruments of chastisement, but the spirit in which they executed this office has provoked his wrath. He designed only to inflict a slight chastisement, but they rioted in the sufferings of his people with wanton cruelty. They mocked their sorrows and taunted them with their abandonment. Hence God will punish these heathen, and will bestow mercy on his people, cause the temple to be built, the city to be enlarged, and prosperity to return to the land.

These predictions were not merely promises of temporal prosperity, such as the theocratic people received in the times of Ezra, Nehemiah, and the Maccabees; but of that better prosperity which took place when the spiritual temple was laid on the chief corner stone, and its stately proportions, all garnished with prophets, apostles and martyrs, went slowly up, preparing for its culmination in the New Jerusalem that shall descend from

15 And I am very sore displeased with the heathen *that are* at ease : for I was but a little displeased, and they helped forward the affliction.

16 Therefore thus saith the LORD ; I

am returned to Jerusalem with mercies: mine house shall be built in it, saith the LORD of hosts, and a line shall be stretched forth upon Jerusalem.

17 Cry yet, saying, Thus saith the

heaven as a bride prepared for her husband. Literally they were fulfilled, but they have a wider fulfilment yet in progress. The threatenings against God's enemies have been fulfilled in like manner. It seemed as vain a fulmination of displeasure for an obscure Jew, amid the ruins of Jerusalem, to predict calamity to magnificent Babylon, as for some humble preacher in our mountains to utter threats against London or Paris. Yet this Jew uttered the word of Jehovah, and the elements of ruin, in their remotest lurking-places, heard the summons, and came up each on its mission of destruction. And now, all that remains of Babylon is a heap of desolation, whilst the Church is lengthening her cords and strengthening her stakes to fill the whole earth. Hence, all that this vision predicted has thus far been fulfilled, a guarantee of a yet ampler fulfilment in the future.

PRACTICAL INFERENCES.

As the Jewish people are usually regarded by the prophet in their theocratic character, as the form in which the Church then existed, the general doctrines of these visions are applicable to the Church in every form in which she exists. Some of these doctrines as set forth in this vision are,—

(1.) The Church is externally an humble and lowly thing, neglected, often despised by the gay and wicked world, a grove of myrtles, rather than the cedars of Lebanon, (v. 8.)

(2.) She has, however, an unseen glory that the world knows not of ; for Christ dwells in her midst, full of love, invested with all power, sending his angel messengers to do his work, and preparing everything for her final triumph, (v. 8, 9.)

(3.) The hour of darkest desolation to the Church, and of haughtiest triumph to her enemies, is often the very hour when God begins his work of judgment on the one, and returning mercy on the other, (v. 11.)

(4.) Christ intercedes for his people, when they need it most, and his intercession is always prevalent, (v. 12, 13.)

(5.) God will have all our hearts, for he is jealous of sharing his glory with another, (v. 14.)

(6.) God often uses instruments to chastise his people, which, when he has done with them, he breaks and casts into the fire, (v. 15.)

(7.) The Church of God shall yet triumph over every obstacle, and vanquish every foe, (v. 16.)

(8.) The promises and threatenings of God, though slow, are sure. They have eternity for the range of their fulfilment, (v. 17.)

(9.) The head of the Church is at once human and divine. He is called here "a man," v. 8, and the "Angel of Jehovah," v. 12. But the Angel of Jehovah is a Divine person, as appears from comparing Gen.

18 ¶ Then lifted I up mine eyes, and saw, and behold four horns.

19 And I said unto the angel that talked with me, What *be* these? and he answered me, These *are* the horns which have scattered Judah, Israel, and Jerusalem.

16 : 7 with v. 13 ; Gen. 22 : 11 with v. 12, &c. Even Gesenius admits this, and the Babylonish Talmud declares that "this man is no other than the Holy One." But if divine and human, he must be God and man in one person.

VISION II.

CHAPTER 1: 18—21.—*The four horns and four artificers.*

ANALYSIS.

I. Four horns appear, symbolizing the various enemies of God's people, (v. 18, 19.)

II. Four artificers appear, symbolizing the fact that God had provided a deliverance for every variety of threatening, (v. 20, 21.)

V. 18—21. "And I lifted up mine eyes, and saw, and behold four horns. And I said unto the angel that talked with me, 'What are these?' And he answered me, 'These are the horns that have scattered Judah, Israel and Jerusalem.' And Jehovah showed me four artificers. And I said, 'What do these come to do?' And he replied, saying, 'These are the horns that have scattered Judah, so that a man could not lift up his head; but these are come to terrify them, to cast out the horns of the nations, which lifted up the horn over the land of Judah to scatter it.'"

THE meaning of this vision is by no means obscure. Among the Orientals a horn was the symbol of power. Being a pastoral people, and finding the strongest of the herd always furnished with horns, the horn became

20 And the LORD shewed me four carpenters.

21 Then said I, What come these to do? And he spake, saying, These *are* the horns which have scattered Judah, so that no man did lift up his head : but these are come to fray them, to cast out the horns of the Gentiles, which lifted up *their* horn over the land of Judah to scatter it.

the natural symbol of power and pride. To lift up the horn, was to be proud of conscious strength ; to have horns coming out of the hands, was to have power in the hands, &c. The number four has given rise to many fanciful conjectures, but undoubtedly refers to the four cardinal points of the compass, which include every possible direction, and so represent all possible enemies. Wherever the people of God turned, there was a power to oppose them. Such was the condition of the Jews then, with the Assyrian, Chaldean and Samaritan on the north, the Egyptian on the south, the Philistine on the west, and the Ammonite and Moabite on the east, they were encircled with foes.

But there also appeared four artificers, whether carpenters or smiths does not appear from the original, and depends on whether the horns were wooden or metallic, a fact not stated. But their office was to break the horns in pieces. The gist of the vision lies in the coincidence of the numbers of the artificers and horns. For every horn there was a cleaving artificer to beat it down ; for every enemy there was an antagonizing instrument to counteract it, already provided by God. Hence, although on all sides there were enemies to oppose the erection of the temple, and the completion of the city, there was provided by God a neutralizing and counteracting power adequate to destroy them all.

CHAPTER II.

THE event has verified the prediction. The temple went up, and the city was builded, in spite of all the efforts of opposing enemies, and now those enemies have passed away, and their gorgeous cities are but heaps of desolation. In its narrowest scope, therefore, the vision has been verified, and the promise intended to encourage the lingering people in erecting the temple has been fulfilled. But its sweep was much wider than the Jews, considered in their national capacity. It referred to them as the theocracy, and hence these promises are made to the Church, and declare the great truth that the gates of hell shall never prevail against her. Such has been the fact thus far, and such will it ever be, for he that is with her is more than they that are against her. For every evil there is a remedy ; for every enemy a deliverer. The evil will be allowed to come, and the enemy to assail, but at the appointed hour, the fraying artificer shall come forth to neutralize the one and vanquish the other.

PRACTICAL INFERENCES.

(1.) The Church of God has always been surrounded with enemies, and will be until the last enemy is destroyed by her head, (v. 18, 19.)

(2.) She can never perish, for more are they that are with her, than they that are against her, (v. 20, 21.)

1 I lifted up mine eyes again, and looked, and behold a man with a measuring line in his hand.

2 Then said I, Whither goest thou? And he said unto me, To measure Jerusalem, to see what *is* the breadth thereof, and what *is* the length thereof.

3. And behold, the angel that talked with me went forth, and another angel went out to meet him,

4. And said unto him, Run, speak to this young man, saying, Jerusalem shall be inhabited *as* towns without walls for the multitude of men and cattle therein :

VISION III.

CHAPTER 2.—*The man with the measuring line.*

ANALYSIS.

I. A man is seen with a measuring line, symbolizing the fact that the boundaries of the Church were then to be declared, (v. 1—3.)

II. The future enlargement of the Church promised, under the fact that Jerusalem would spread beyond her walls into the country, (v. 4, 5.)

III. In view of this enlargement the exiles are called home, (v. 6, 7;) Divine protection promised, (v. 8, 9;) and the conversion of the world predicted as a consequence of God's dwelling in the midst of his people, (v. 10—13.)

V. 1, 2. "And I lifted up mine eyes, and looked and behold a man, and in his hand a measuring line. And I said, ' Where art thou going ?' And he said unto me, ' To measure Jerusalem, to see what is its breadth, and what is its length.' "

THE apparatus of this vision is very simple and easily understood. A man is seen with a measuring line, as in Ezek. 40 : 1—3, who is probably the angel of the covenant, the Son of God, who goes forth to measure Jerusalem. This indicates at once that the Church should be enlarged, and that Christ was to be the author and definer of this enlargement. The interpreting

5 For I, saith the LORD, will be unto her a wall of fire round about, and will be the glory in the midst of her.

6 ¶ Ho, ho, *come forth*, and flee from the land of the north, saith the LORD : for I have spread you abroad as the

angel having left him was met by another messenger from the measuring angel, who directed him to run to Zechariah, indicating thus the spirit with which God's messengers serve him. Those who would do God's will aright must neither crawl, nor walk, but run with eager alacrity. Zechariah is called a young man, not only on account of his age, but also in allusion to his subordinate relation to the angels, as παὶς, *puer*, *garçon*, and boy, are used in their respective languages to indicate relation rather than age, being applied often to servants who have long passed the years of boyhood. The substance of this communication is that Jerusalem shall be enlarged, and attain a high measure of prosperity, and that her enemies shall be overthrown.

V. 3, 4. "And behold, the angel that talked with me went forth, and another angel came out to meet him, And said unto him, Run, speak to this young man, (*Zechariah*,) saying, Jerusalem shall inhabit villages. For the multitude of men and cattle in her midst."

Henderson and some of the recent German expositors, such as Hitzig, Maurer and Ewald, maintain that "the young man" is the man with the measuring line ; others think that it was the interpreting angel. But as it was a communication intended for the prophet, we prefer with most interpreters to take Zechariah as the person described.

" Jerusalem shall inhabit villages," *i. e.* shall so spread out as to extend beyond her narrow walls, and reach

four winds of the heaven, saith the   7 Deliver thyself, O Zion, that dwell
Lord.   est *with* the daughter of Babylon.

the adjacent villages : and her security shall be such
that she shall not need the protection of walls to guard
her from the incursion of enemies.   Literally, this was
fulfilled in the subsequent great growth of the city. But
its reference was mainly to the Church of which Jerusalem was but the theocratic symbol.   The narrow walls
of the Mosaic forms were to be thrown down, and her
limits extended to those who were then beyond these
boundaries, and this with the most perfect safety and
advantage.   It is at least a curious coincidence that
when this enlargement actually did take place, the
dwellers in villages (*pagani*) became synonymous with
those to whom heathenism had been driven gradually
from the centres of population, until at last having
reached and converted these very *paganos* (pagans),
Jerusalem in very deed inhabited the villages.

V. 5. "And I will be to her, saith Jehovah, a wall of fire around,
and for a glory will I be in her midst."

But is there not something unsafe in this unwalled
extension ? Is there not danger in simplifying the
forms of the spiritual Jerusalem, as well as in extending
beyond the walls of the literal Jerusalem ? The answer
is no! for (v. 5) God will be to her a wall without, and
a glory within, furnishing a security and a splendor far
more glorious than any external munitions.   Hence
they might labor for that extension whether in the
narrower form of the work then before them, or the

8 For thus saith the LORD of hosts :
After the glory hath he sent me unto
the nations which spoiled you : for he

that toucheth you, toucheth the apple
of his eye.
9 For behold, I will shake my hand

wider form of that enlargement that was yet future, with unwavering confidence and hope.

V. 6, 7. "Ho ! Ho ! fly then from the north country, saith Jehovah, for as the four winds of heaven have I scattered you, saith Jehovah. O Zion ! deliver thyself, thou that dwellest with the daughter of Babylon."

As there were yet a number of Jews in Babylon, the angel urges them to return, first, because of the judgments to come on Babylon, ("the land of the North,") and secondly, because of the blessings to come on Jerusalem. "As the four winds," &c., means, not that God had scattered the Jews *to* the four winds, but *as* the four winds scatter, *i. e.* violently and afar off. Zion means the Jews yet remaining who are urged to leave Babylon before the assault of Darius, that soon afterwards occurred. "Daughter of Babylon" means simply Babylon, see Isa. 1 : 8 ; Ps. 9 : 14 ; Ps. 137 : 8.

V. 8. "For thus saith Jehovah of Hosts : after the glory hath he sent me to the nations that spoiled you, for he that toucheth you, toucheth the pupil of his own eye."

The phrase "after the glory" has received several expositions. Blayney, Newcome, Hitzig, Maurer, and others, understand it to mean that God had sent the speaker after the glory to obtain it, but "after" is always used as an adverb of place or time, and not as a preposition. Hence it is better with Calvin, Henderson, and others, to make it refer to the glory in v. 5,

upon them, and they shall be a spoil to
their servants : and ye shall know that
the LORD of hosts hath sent me.

10 ¶ Sing and rejoice, O daughter

of Zion : for lo, I come, and I will
dwell in the midst of thee, saith the
LORD.

and declare that after this glory, *i. e.* not only in point
of time, but in point of fact, *besides* this glory, God has
sent me to punish your enemies.   In other words, I am
not only a glory to you, but also an avenger upon your
enemies.   The speaker is the Divine angel, or the Son
of God.   The image of the last clause is both expressive
and beautiful.   Henderson refers the pronominal suffix
to God, representing the Jewish people as the apple of
his own eye, and Calvin favors that view.   Most interpreters refer it to the enemy.

V. 9. " For, behold, I will shake my hand (*fist*) over them, and they
shall be a spoil to their own servants ; and ye shall acknowledge
that Jehovah of Hosts hath sent me."

V. 9 repeats the threat of v. 8, using a gesture of
menace, and predicts that they should be a spoil to their
servants, which was literally fulfilled when the Persians
conquered Babylon, and ruled where they once served,
and shall yet be more widely fulfilled in God's subjugation of all his enemies.

V. 10. " Sing and rejoice, O daughter of Zion, for behold I come ;
and I will dwell in thy midst, saith Jehovah."

V. 10 predicts that coming of the covenant angel
that first took place in the incarnation, and shall be
more perfectly fulfilled only when he comes the second
time without sin to salvation.   The language of this
verse is almost identical with that of ch. 9 : 9, that

11 And many nations shall be join- be my people : and I will dwell in the
ed to the LORD in that day, and shall midst of thee, and thou shalt know

unquestionably refers to the incarnation. Even Kimchi
refers this verse to the Messiah.

V. 11. "And many nations shall be joined to Jehovah in that
day, shall be to me for a people, and I will dwell in the midst of
them, and thou shalt know that Jehovah of Hosts hath sent me
unto thee."

V. 11 announces the conversion of the Gentiles, and
the general recognition that shall be made of Christ's
messianic character and divine mission.

V. 12. "And Jehovah shall inherit Judah his portion, in a land
of holiness, and shall choose again Jerusalem."

V. 12 proclaims the future restoration of the Jews to
their ancient relation to God.

V. 13. "Be silent, all flesh, before Jehovah, because he is arisen
from the habitation of his holiness."

V. 13 is a grand peroration, in which the prophet
loses sight of the present and addresses the distant future. God seems to be slumbering and delaying his
judgments, and hence men are growing bold and impi-
ous. But see ! he arises like a giant refreshed with
slumber, and comes forth to do his strange and terrible
work. Be silent, therefore, all flesh, before this dread
apparition !

PRACTICAL INFERENCES.

(1.) Although Zion has not yet lengthened her cords
and widened her stakes to her appointed limits, yet the
measuring line has gone forth that gives her bounds to be

that the LORD of hosts hath sent me unto thee.

12 And the LORD shall inherit Judah his portion in the holy land, and shall choose Jerusalem again.

13 Be silent, O all flesh, before the LORD : for he is raised up out of his holy habitation.

the habitable earth. Hence, if this future extension was a motive to the Jew, in his work of rearing the temple of wood and stone, much more is it to us in our work of erecting the great spiritual temple on the foundation, Jesus Christ, (v. 1—4.)

(2.) We learn here the true glory of the Church. It is not in any external pomp or power, of any kind ; not in frowning battlements, either of temporal or spiritual pretensions ; not in rites and ceremonies, however moss-grown and venerable ; not in splendid cathedrals and gorgeous vestments, and the swell of music, and the glitter of eloquence, but in the indwelling glory of the invisible God. Her outward rites and ceremonies, therefore, should only be like what the earth's atmosphere is to the rays of the sun, a pure, transparent medium of transmission, (v. 5.)

(3.) The punishment of the wicked as truly declares the glory of God as the salvation of the righteous, (v. 8.)

(4.) The wicked shall ultimately be the slaves of their own lusts, those appetites and passions that were designed to be merely their obedient servants, shall become their tormenting and inexorable tyrants, (v. 9.)

(5.) The incarnation of Christ, and his indwelling in the Church, are grounds of the highest joy, (v. 10.)

(6.) Christ is a divine Saviour. In v. 10, 11, we have

one Jehovah sending another, and the Jehovah sent is identified with the angel of the covenant, who was to come and dwell in the Church, whom we know to be Christ. Hence, unless there are two distinct Jehovahs, one divine and the other not, Christ, the Jehovah angel of this passage is divine.

(7.) The Church of God shall cover the earth, and become in fact what it is in right, the mightiest agency in human history. Though now feeble and despised, she shall one day include many nations, and every knee shall bow and every tongue confess that Jesus is Lord to the glory of God the Father, (v. 11.)

(8.) Delay of punishment is no proof of impunity. God often seems to be asleep, but he is only awaiting the appointed time, but in the end, when all seems as it was from the foundation of the world, the herald cry shall go forth, be silent, O earth, for Jehovah is aroused to his terrible work, and the day of his wrath is come. Let men kiss the Son whilst he is yet in the way, before his anger is kindled but a little, and they perish before him like stubble before the whirlwind of flames.

1 And he shewed me Joshua the high priest standing before the angel of the LORD, and Satan standing at his right hand to resist him.

VISION IV.

CHAP. 3.—*Joshua the High Priest before the Angel of* JEHOVAH.

ANALYSIS.

I. Joshua, in his representative character, stands before the Divine angel in filthy garments, with Satan accusing him. The filthy garments, symbolical of sin in the people, are removed, and clean ones given in their place, symbolical of pardon, (v. 1—5.)

II. A charge and promise given to him in this capacity, (v. 6, 7;) a promise of the Messiah, and a blessing to the Church as a consequence of his coming, (v. 8—10.)

V. 1. "And he showed me Joshua, the high priest, standing before the angel of Jehovah, and Satan standing at his right hand to accuse him."

THIS vision is of less obvious interpretation than the preceding, perhaps for the reason that its truth lies nearer the deepest throbbings of the human heart. A sense of sin, and a feeling of hopeless ill-desert, are among the deepest emotions of a heart that has been touched by the Holy Spirit. This is the ever-recurring state of the human heart, both individually and collectively, because it rests on the ever-during relations that connect man and God. A sense of sin fairly awakened produces despair, if we are thrown back on the resources of reason. We cannot hope in God, for we tremble before his justice. Thus it was with the Jewish church at this time. They felt that they had sinned, and hence had no

2 And the LORD said unto Satan, The LORD rebuke thee, O Satan ; even the LORD that hath chosen Jerusalem re- buke thee : *is* not this a brand plucked out of the fire ?

ground in themselves to hope for God's favor. They knew that their priests had also been unfaithful, and hence they had no hope in them. Why then go forward with the temple, when both priest and people must defile rather than hallow its courts? Was it not presumption to expect that their labor would be accepted? These were the suggestions of Satan to their hearts, to deter them from their work, suggestions with which the people of God are, alas! too familiar to this day. God will not accept so vile and faithless a heart, so lame and mutilated a service as you render him, says the tempter, therefore you had better abandon it all, and enjoy sin at least if you cannot enjoy holiness. This brings us to the heart of the vision. It is designed to show the people of God, that their personal demerit is no ground for distrusting the mercy of God, for he receives them not because of their own righteousness, but that of another ; and that at this particular period, the unworthiness of the priesthood was no reason for their destruction and the overthrow of the temple, as they were typical, and the end of their institution was not yet served. Such is the general purport of it.

The scene is laid in the temple. Joshua the high priest is seen standing before the Divine angel performing the functions of his office. He is not, as some suppose, arraigned for trial, with Satan as his accuser, but is standing in his official character to represent the

E

3 Now Jôshua was clothed with filthy garments, and stood before the angel.

4 And he answered and spake unto those that stood before him, saying, Take away the filthy garments from

people and the priesthood. He represents the people in his character as priest, and the priesthood in his character as high priest. This representative character must be carefully noted, as it contains the essence of the vision. He stands as the representative of the theocratic people, and the priestly order as then existing. But he is clothed in filthy garments, the common symbol of sin. Both people and priesthood feel that they are sinful and unworthy, and hence fear to hope for a blessing from a holy God on their labors. Satan then stands to accuse them in the person of their representative, representing thus these suggestions of the tempter to which we have alluded. "You are not fit to appear before God, and there is nothing in you that can be pleasing to him, therefore abandon his service, which you are only polluting, and act out your character in your conduct, by indulging openly in sin and rebellion."

V. 2. "And Jehovah said to Satan. Jehovah rebuke thee, O Satan! Jehovah rebuke thee! he that chooses Jerusalem! Is not this a brand plucked from the fire?"

Here, then, God gives his answer to the tempter. "Begone, false fiend! Blacken not the glorious gospel by such lying suggestions! It is not Jerusalem that chooses Jehovah, but Jehovah that chooses Jerusalem. It is not the burning brand that plucks the hand, but the hand that plucks it. Hence though Jerusalem, the people of God, whom Joshua represents, are all covered

him. And unto him he said, Behold, from thee, and I will clothe thee witl·
I have caused thine iniquity to pass change of raiment.

with sin as with a garment, I have chosen them in spite
of this sin, not that they should continue in it, but that
they should be freed from it."

V. 3, 4. "And Joshua was clothed in filthy garments and stood
before the angel. And he answered and spake to those who stood
before him, saying, Take the filthy garments away from him ; and
he said to him, (*Joshua*) Behold I take away from thee thy sins,
and they shall clothe thee with festal garments."

Then to show that it was not their righteousness but
another's that was the ground of their acceptance, and
that it was not to encourage them in sin, but to remove
it, the divine angel commanded, v. 4, that these filthy
garments (the symbol of sin) should be removed, and
festal robes (the symbol of imputed righteousness)
should be put on him, thus setting forth the great and
consoling doctrine of a gratuitous justification because
of the merits of the Redeemer. This and this alone can
comfort the heart of the penitent, whether a solitary
monk, weeping and striving in the convent of Erfurth,
or a desponding people brooding in discouragement
over the ruins of Jerusalem.

V. 5. " Then I said, let them place a clean tiara upon his head ;
and they placed a clean tiara upon his head, and they put garments
upon him, and the angel of Jehovah was (*still*) standing (*there.*)"

Here, then, the prophet interposes, (v. 5,) to bring to
view the second main thought of the vision. The first
had reference to Joshua representing the whole people,
who are assured that God will not destroy them because

5 And I said, Let them set a fair mitre upon his head. So they set a fair mitre upon his head, and clothed him with garments. And the angel of the LORD stood by.

6 And the angel of the LORD protested unto Joshua, saying,

of their unworthiness. But now for their more immediate comfort, to quell their fears as to the priesthood, the prophet desires a token to be given of the continuance and official purity of this order, and hence asks that a clean tiara or priestly mitre be placed on his head, to indicate that this purification was complete, both in its nature and in its extent. This was done (v. 5) whilst the angel of the Lord was standing there, to show his approval of, and interest in this process.

V. 6, 7. "And the angel of Jehovah answered to Joshua, saying, Thus saith Jehovah of Hosts, If thou wilt walk in my ways, and if thou wilt keep my laws, thou shalt judge my house, and also keep my courts, and I will give thee guides among these that are standing here."

V. 6, 7, show the conditions annexed to this forgiveness. It was a salvation *from* sin, not *in* it ; and connected with obedience. This obedience, then, was connected with a promise of reward. This reward was judging God's house and guarding his courts, which included supreme authority in sacred things, such as was assigned to the priesthood. מַהְלְכִים is taken by Ackermann, Maurer, Rosenmüller, Hitzig, Ewald, and others, as the plural of the noun מַהֲלָךְ, meaning *walks* or *walking places ;* but this gives no satisfactory sense. It is therefore better with Henderson, Hengstenberg, and some of the older interpreters, to take it as the Chaldaic form of the Hiphil participle of הָלַךְ, meaning " *those*

7 Thus saith the LORD of hosts ; If thou wilt walk in my ways, and if thou wilt keep my charge, then thou shalt also judge my house, and shalt also keep my courts, and I will give thee places to walk among these that stand by.

8 Hear now, O Joshua, the high

who cause to go," or "walk," i. e. *guides*.   Those who are thus alluded to were the angels.   It is therefore a promise of angelic aid and ministry similar to Ps. 91 : 11, 12, and parallel passages.   The cheering encouragement of this every trembling heart can feel.

V. 8. "Hear, I beseech thee, O Joshua, the high priest, thou and thy colleagues who sit before thee, for men of omen are they: for behold I bring my servant, BRANCH."

V. 8 presents another reason for encouragement. The priesthood would not be destroyed because of its typical character.   *Men of omen*, are men who shadow forth something future, (see Isa. 8 : 18, 20 : 3 ;) in other words, typical men, whose office foreshadows something to come.   What this was is then declared, "my servant, BRANCH."   These are undoubted appellations of the Messiah.   He is called " servant " in such passages as, Isa. 42 : 1, 49 : 3, 50 : 10 ; Ezek. 34 : 23, &c. ; and *Branch*, in Jer. 23 : 5, 33 : 15.   This designation is given to him to indicate his original obscurity, and the gradual development of his character.   The type then would continue until the coming of the anti-type, the order foretokening the Messiah would not cease until he came, and hence they could go on in the erection of the temple, in which these priests were to minister.

The notion of some of the Jewish, and a few Christian interpreters, that the person predicted under the

priest, thou and thy fellows that sit before thee : for they *are* men wondered at : for behold, I will bring forth my servant The BRANCH.

9 For behold the stone that I have laid before Joshua; upon one stone *shall be* seven eyes : behold, I will engrave the graving thereof, saith the

name of Branch was Zerubbabel, is wholly untenable, for the Branch had not yet appeared, whilst Zerubbabel had. Even Maurer, Hitzig, and similar critics, concede that the Messiah is here meant.

V. 9. " For behold the stone which I have laid before Joshua, upon this one stone shall there be seven eyes ; behold, carving I will carve it, saith Jehovah of Hosts, and I will remove the sin of the land in one day."

V. 9 gives the reason for the fulfilment of this glorious promise. Everything seemed so desolate, that there was no hope of such a blessing as the coming of the Messiah. God declares that although his people were thus obscure and desolate, he had never lost sight of them. He represents his people, or the theocracy, by a stone, a *single* stone (*Ehad*), lying before Joshua, as if worthless. But he says that on this one stone are " seven eyes." Seven being the number of perfection, the seven eyes represent the all-seeing eye of Jehovah, and show the sleepless regard which he bestows upon his Church. The image of a stone was selected, because the main work of the theocratic people then was the erection of a temple. God assures them that he has not cast it aside, but would yet polish and chisel it, and make it suitable for its glorious destiny. The removal of sin " in one day," refers to the perfection of the atonement to be made by the Messiah, which needs not daily

LORD of hosts, and I will remove the iniquity of that land in one day.

10 In that day. saith the LORD of hosts, shall ye call every man his neighbor under the vine and under the fig tree.

repetition like the sacrifices of the priesthood, but " by one offering he perfected forever them that are sanctified." Heb. 10 : 14.   Henderson refers " the stone" to the literal foundation of the temple, but with a very needless restriction and literality.   God did not carve that stone, and if one part of the verse is figurative, so must be the other.

V. 10. " In that day, saith Jehovah of Hosts, ye shall call every man to his neighbor, under the vine and under the fig-tree."

V. 10 refers to the security and peace that should reign in the Messianic period, first in the heart of the penitent believer, then in the bosom of the faithful Church, and then at last in the glories of the latter day and heavenly rest. 2 Kings 18 : 31 shows that this was a familiar image of prosperity and peace.   Thus, as in all these visions, the prophet connects the present with the future, the passing and perishing with the unchanging and eternal.

PRACTICAL INFERENCES.

(1.) The divinity of Christ.   The Jehovah angel of v. 1 is called Jehovah in v. 2, and this Jehovah angel, as appears from other passages, especially Haggai 2 : 6, 7, and Malachi 3 : 1, compared with Mark 1 : 2, we know to be Jesus Christ.

(2.) Satan's temptations are never so subtle or so powerful as when they assume the form of penitence and humility.   But the greatness of our sin only magnifies the greatness of the mercy that pardons it.

(3.) The origin of our salvation and the ground of our hope are in the love and grace of God, and not in our own worthiness or merit, (v. 2.)

(4.) We are saved by the imputed righteousness of Christ and not by our own merits, (v. 4.)

(5.) A gratuitous justification furnishes no excuse for inaction and sin, but leads to more entire obedience, (v. 7.)

(6.) Fidelity in God's service shall be gloriously rewarded, (v. 7.)

(7.) Angelic guidance shall be given to the faithful people of God, (v. 7.)

(8.) The ceremonial system of the O. T. typified Christ, (v. 8.)

(9.) The atonement of Christ is perfect, and needs no addition of penances or human merits, (v. 9.)

(10.) The tendency of true religion is toward peace and prosperity, to men individually and collectively, (v. 10.)

1 And the angel that talked with me came again, and waked me, as a man that is wakened out of his sleep,

2 And said unto me, What seest thou ? And I said, I have looked, and behold a candlestick all *of* gold, with a bowl upon the top of it, and his sev-

en lamps thereon, and seven pipes to the seven lamps, which *are* upon the top thereof :

3 And two olive trees by it, one upon the right *side* of the bowl, and the other upon the left *side* thereof.

4 So I answered and spake to the

Vision V.

CHAPTER 4.—*The Golden Candlestick, and the two Olive Trees.*

ANALYSIS.

I. A golden candlestick symbolizes the theocracy, and two olive trees the source of its strength. The prophet asks the meaning of the vision, (v. 1—5.)

II. The teaching of the vision : that all the work of the Church was to be done by the supply of divine strength, and hence all obstacles would vanish, (v. 6—11.)

III. The explanation of the various parts of the symbolical vision, (v. 12—14.)

V. 1—6. "And the angel who spoke with me returned, and awaked me as a man who is awaked from his sleep : and he said unto me, 'What seest thou ?' And I said, 'I have looked and behold a candlestick all of gold, and a bowl on the top of it, and its seven lamps upon it, and seven tubes to each lamp on the top of it : and two olive trees, one on the right hand of the bowl, and one on the left hand.' And I answered and spake to the angel that talked with me, saying, 'What are these, my lord ?' Then the angel that talked with me answered and said unto me, 'Dost thou not know what these are ?' And I said, 'No, my lord.' Then he answered and spake unto me, saying, 'This is the word of Jehovah unto Zerubbabel, saying, Not by might, and not by power, but by my spirit, saith Jehovah of Hosts.' "

A PAUSE seems to have occurred after the preceding vision, and the prophet, for a time, to have relapsed

angel that talked with me, saying, What *are* these, my lord ?

5 Then the angel that talked with me answered and said unto me, Knowest thou not what these be ? and I said, No, my lord.

6 Then he answered and spake unto me, saying, This *is* the word of the LORD unto Zerubbabel, saying, Not by might, not by power, but by my Spirit, saith the LORD of hosts.

7 Who *art* thou, O great mountain ? before Zerubbabel *thou shalt become* a plain : and he shall bring forth the headstone *thereof with* shoutings, *crying*, Grace, grace unto it.

into his ordinary and normal state. This state compared with the prophetic ecstacy, was as sleep to waking ; the ordinary state of the soul being so insensible to those impressions that were made upon it in the prophetic condition. But he was soon roused from that state by the angel and bidden to look. He saw a candlestick of gold with a bowl on the top, having seven lamps, and each lamp furnished with seven feeding tubes, making forty-nine in all, and two olive trees standing beside the candlestick, from the two crowded branches of which the clustering olives were pouring a constant supply of golden colored oil into tubes that led into the bowl. The prophet inquires into the meaning of this vision, and after some delay is told, (v. 6,) that it conveys the truth that in carrying on the work of the Church, it is not by human power that it is either to be advanced or retarded, but by the strength of God.

The candlestick represented the Theocracy, the Church of God, an image of great beauty, showing her mission to be a light-bearer in a dark world. The material, gold, indicated the purity, preciousness and indestructibleness of all that pertained to her. The seven lamps, and seven times seven tubes, indicated, by the use of the

8 Moreover the word of the LORD came unto me, saying,

9 The hands of Zerubbabel have laid the foundation of this house ; his hands shall also finish it ; and thou shalt know that the LORD of hosts hath sent me unto you.

10 For who hath despised the day of small things ? for they shall rejoice, and shall see the plummet in the hand of Zerubbabel *with* those seven ; they *are* the eyes of the LORD, which run to and fro through the whole earth.

number of perfection, the manifold modes by which her light was to be given out, and the manifold modes by which grace was to be imparted. The olive trees represented the source of that grace, the Spirit of God, from whom comes forth all supplies of strength for the Church.

Here, then, were these lamps burning continually, lamps that man's hand did not make, and does not feed, and yet supplied from a source that is exhaustless, the living trees that stand beside the candlestick. Now, if the strength to do God's work comes from God, the weakness of man is no obstacle, for when he is weak then is he strong. Zerubbabel may have but few visible resources, but the work was one that after all was to be completed by God, and not by man, and however feeble the Church might seem to be, there was more for her than against her. Hence, as the Jew gazed on this ceaseless flow of strength and grace, he could forget the feebleness of man in the unfailing supply of the power of God.

V. 7. "Who art thou, thou great mountain before Zerubbabel ? Be a plain ! He shall bring forth the top-stone with shoutings, Grace ! Grace unto it."

But there were obstacles in the way, like a great

11 ¶ Then answered I, and said unto him, What *are* these two olive trees upon the right *side* of the candlestick and upon the left *side* thereof?

mountain. These obstacles should be prostrated like a plain before him, (v. 7,) so that the work should be completed, the top-stone laid, and it should be seen that all was of grace. Hence they should not falter in the work before them.

V. 8—11. "And the word of Jehovah came unto me saying, The hands of Zerubbabel have founded this house, and his hands shall finish it, and thou shalt know that Jehovah of Hosts hath sent me unto you. For who will despise the day of small things? For they shall rejoice and see the plummet in the hand of Zerubbabel, these seven eyes of Jehovah, they run to and fro in the whole earth."

V. 8, 9, contain positive assurances that the temple shall be finished by Zerubbabel, and not left unfinished as it had been before, by the intrigues of their enemies.

V. 10 rebukes them for despising the feebleness of the Church in external resources, and overlooking her true glory. That glory lay in the fact that God's eye (the seven eyes) was upon her in love, and although those eyes see all that is in the earth, the most mighty and most magnificent, yet they see nothing that is mighty enough to destroy the Church, or magnificent enough to eclipse her true glory. The plummet (*stone of tin*, Heb.) in the hand of Zerubbabel indicated that the work was there going forward to completion.

V. 12—14. "And I answered and said unto him, 'What are these two olive trees on the right hand of the candlestick, and on the left?' And I answered again and said unto him, 'What are the two olive branches which through the tubes of gold pour out the

12 And I answered again, and said unto him, What *be these* two olive branches which through the two gold-en pipes empty the golden *oil* out of themselves?

13 And he answered me and said, golden oil from themselves?' And he answered unto me, saying, 'Knowest thou not what these are?' And I said, 'No, my lord.' 'These are the two sons of oil, that stand by the Lord of the whole earth.'"

The meaning of the olive trees, or as the prophet sees more distinctly, of the two olive branches, is next explained. The two questions are asked, and the first left unanswered in vs. 11, 12, to draw special attention to the duality of the olive branches. To what does this refer? The answer is, to the two anointed ones that minister before God. Who are these? They refer to some standing channel of blessing from God, and are alluded to again in Rev. 11: 3, 4, in terms that cannot be mistaken. Without entering at length into the reasons for the opinion, we simply affirm that they refer to a duality of gracious manifestation from God, corresponding to a duality of necessity in the nature of man. There are two grand evils to be overcome, guilt and pollution, and they demand two standing sources of blessing, the one to remove the guilt by atonement, the other to remove the power of sin by giving a higher power of holiness. These two sources are embodied in two official forms, the only two that were connected with the theocracy as permanent elements, the sacerdotal and regal orders. They existed once in Melchisedek, but were ever afterwards divided, as in Moses and Aaron, Joshua and Zerubbabel, &c., &c., until the

Knowest thou not what these *be?* And
I said, No, my lord.

14 Then said he, These *are* the two

anointed ones, that stand by the Lord
of the whole earth.

time of the Messiah, who again combined them in his
own person, and who by his work, made his people
kings and priests unto God. This duality marked all
the manifestations of God, for it rested on a deep necessity of human nature, and it was then embodied in the
persons of Joshua and Zerubbabel. Since then they
were so essential to the theocracy, the people need not
suppose that God would allow them to perish, but
would continue them in existence until he should come
who was a priest after the order of Melchisedek.

PRACTICAL INFERENCES.

(1.) The Church is the same under both dispensations, for the promises made to her then are only fulfilling now, showing that then and now she was the
same Church. The candlestick is the same, though the
tubes may be changed, and the Church is the same,
though her official channels be totally altered.

(2.) The Church is the light of the world, and only as
Christians show forth their light are they fulfilling their
duty, (v. 1—3.)

(3.) God has provided an unfailing source of strength
for his people. Their supply comes not from a dead
reservoir of oil, but a living olive tree, that is ever
drawing from the rich earth its generous furnishings,
and then distilling them by seven pipes, a perfect

number, to those who are to be burning and shining lights, (v. 1—3.)

(4.) The whole work of religion in the heart of the individual, and throughout the world, is of grace. Christ is at once the corner-stone and the cope-stone of the Church; and as he was greeted with shoutings of "grace!" when he came the first time, much more shall he when he comes the second time, without sin to salvation, (v. 7.)

(5.) We are prone to judge of God's work by man's standard; and because we see but a narrow stream from the fountain, doubt or deny the river, (v. 9.)

(6.) It is not only unwise, but it is wicked to be disheartened because of the external feebleness of the Church, compared with the work she has to do, and the enemies she has to encounter. God is her strength, her glory and her hope, and to despair of her is to deny God, (v. 10.)

(7.) The doctrine and discipline of the Church, the truth and power that God has lodged in her organization and her ordinances, are still the standing channels through which the spirit pours the oil of grace and strength, and hence should both be kept pure and unclogged, (v. 11—14.)

1 Then I turned, and lifted up mine eyes, and looked, and behold a flying roll.

2 And he said unto me, What seest thou? And I answered, I see a flying roll; the length thereof *is* twenty cubits, and the breadth thereof ten cubits.

3 Then said he unto me, This *is* the

VISION VI.

CHAPTER 5 : 1—4.—*The Flying Roll.*

ANALYSIS.

I. An outstretched roll is seen flying through the air, twenty by ten cubits, (v. 1, 2.)

II. The meaning of the vision. A threatening against all transgressors of either table of the law, (v. 3, 4.)

V. 1—4. "Then I turned and raised my eyes, and looked, and behold a flying roll. And he (*the interpreting angel*) said unto me, 'What dost thou see?' And I said, 'I see a flying roll, in length twenty cubits, and in breadth ten cubits.' Then he said unto me, 'This is the curse that goes forth before the face of the whole land, for every thief shall be cut off according to this side, and every perjurer shall be cut off according to that side. I have caused it to go forth, saith Jehovah of Hosts, and it shall go into the house of the thief, and into the house of him that swears falsely by my name, and it shall dwell in the midst of it, and it consumes their house, and its wood and its stone.'"

THE import of this vision is threatening, to show that the object of the prophet was to produce genuine penitence. The parts are significant. A roll, probably of parchment, is seen, 30 by 15 feet, the exact dimensions of the temple porch, where the law was usually read, showing that it was authoritative in its utterance, and connected with the theocracy. Being a written thing,

curse that goeth forth over the face of the whole earth : for every one that stealeth shall be cut off *as* on this side, according to it; and every one that sweareth shall be cut off *as* on that side, according to it.

4 I will bring it forth, saith the LORD of hosts, and it shall enter into

it showed that its contents were solemnly determined, beyond all escape or repeal. It was flying, to show that its threats were ready to do their work, and descend on every transgressor. It was unrolled, or the dimensions could not have been seen, to show that its warnings were openly proclaimed to all, that none might have an excuse. It was written on both sides, to connect it with the tables of the law, and show its comprehensive character. One side denounced perjury, a sin of the first table, the other stealing, a sin of the second; and both united in every case where a thief took the oath of expurgation to acquit himself of the charge of theft. This hovering curse would descend in every such case into the house of the offender, and consume even its most enduring parts, until it had thoroughly done its work of destruction.

The immediate application of this vision was to those who were neglecting the erection of God's house to build their own, and thus robbing God, and forswearing their obligations to him. On such the prophet declares a curse shall descend, that will make this selfish withholding of their efforts in vain, for the houses they would build should be consumed by God's wrath.

PRACTICAL INFERENCES.

The teaching of this vision is that of the law. It

F

the house of the thief, and into the house of him that sweareth falsely by my name: and it shall remain in the midst of his house, and shall consume it with the timber thereof and the stones thereof.

blazes with the fire and echoes the thunder of Sinai, and tells us that our God is a consuming fire. We learn thus a lesson of instruction to those who have succeeded the prophets of the Old Testament, as the authorized expounders of God's will under the New. It is needful to tell the love of God, to unfold his precious promises, and to utter words of cheer and encouragement. But it is also needful to declare the other aspect of God's character. There is a constant tendency in the human heart to abuse the goodness of God to an encouragement of sin. Hence, ministers of the gospel must declare this portion of God's counsel as well as the other. They must declare to men who are living in neglect of duty, that withholding what is due to God, either in heart or life, is combined robbery and perjury. For those who thus sin, God has prepared a ministry of vengeance. There is something most vivid and appalling in this image of the hovering curse. It flies viewless, and resistless, poising like a falcon over her prey, breathing a ruin the most dire and desolating, and when the blind and hardened offender opens his door to his ill-gotten gains, this mystic roll, with its fire-tracery of wrath, enters into his habitation, and fastening upon his cherished idols, begins its dread work of retribution, and ceases not until the fabric of his guilty life has been totally and irremediably consumed.

5 ¶ Then the angel that talked with me went forth, and said unto me, Lift up now thine eyes, and see what *is* this that goeth forth.

6 And I said, What *is* it? and he said, This *is* an ephah that goeth forth. He said moreover, This *is* their resemblance through all the earth.

Vision VII.

Chapter 5 : 5—11.—*The Woman in the Ephah.*

ANALYSIS.

I. An ephah is seen coming forth, in which a woman was sitting. A talent of lead was raised up and laid on the ephah, which was then lifted up by two winged women and carried into the land of Shinar, (v. 5—11.)

II. The explanation of the vision: that the people for their sins should be carried into a long and distant exile, (v. 8, 11.)

V. 5—11. "Then the angel that talked with me went forth, and said unto me, ' Lift up, I pray thee, thine eyes, and see what this is that goeth forth.' And I said, ' What is this ?' And he said, ' This is the ephah which goeth forth,' and he said, ' This is their appearance in all the land.' And behold a talent of lead was lifted up. ' But this is the woman that is sitting in the midst of the ephah.' And he said, ' This is wickedness.' And he thrust her down into the midst of the ephah, and he cast the stone of lead upon its mouth. And I raised my eyes and saw, and behold two women came out, and the wind in their wings, for they had wings like the wings of a stork, and they raised the ephah between earth and heaven. And I said to the angel that talked with me, ' Where do these carry the ephah ?' And he said unto me, ' To build for it a house in the land of Shinar: and it (*the house*) shall be settled and fixed on its own base.' "

THIS vision, like the preceding, is of a warning character, and somewhat more obscure in its symbolical apparatus. A dim outline rises to the eye of the prophet,

7 And behold, there was lifted up a talent of lead : and this *is* a woman that sitteth in the midst of the ephah.

8 And he said, This *is* wickedness.

And he cast it into the midst of the ephah ; and he cast the weight of lead upon the mouth thereof.

9 Then lifted I up mine eyes, and

to which the angel calls his attention, but which be cannot at first distinctly make out.   The angel tells him that it is an ephah, a very common dry measure containing about three pecks.   He then sees a mass of lead containing about a *cwt.*, lifted up above the measure, and on looking more closely he sees a woman in the measure.   This woman is then violently thrust down into the measure, and the mass of lead laid upon its mouth, after which two winged women carry it away into the land of Shinar, where it was to be permanently deposited in a house prepared for it there.

The general meaning of this is to show, that when the measure of the people's wickedness became full, then their punishment should come, and they should again be carried into the land of their enemies in exile, not for seventy years, but for a long time.   As the flying roll symbolized the certainty and completeness of their punishment, so this vision indicated its swiftness and mode.   The ephah is selected simply as a common dry measure, to symbolize the thought that there is a certain measure of sin beyond which the people cannot go with impunity.   The woman sitting in it, represents the Jewish people, by a common figure.   The phrase, "this is their appearance (Heb. *eye*) in all the land," v. 6, simply means, this represents that to which the people are looking, or tending, viz., to fill up the

looked, and behold, there came out
two women, and the wind *was* in their
wings; for they had wings like the
wings of a stork: and they lifted up

measure of their sin, and when they have filled up the
measure of their sin, God will lay upon them their punishment. When the prophet perceives the woman in
the measure, he is told that this is (represents) wickedness, *i. e.* that of the Jewish people. Henderson thinks
that the wickedness here represented was idolatry, and
that the vision predicted the removal of idolatry from
Palestine to Babylon. But there is no reason at all to
limit it thus, but rather the contrary. Idolatry had not
been a sin of the Jews for a century, and would hardly
be represented as an existing thing, as this vision does.
It did not exist in the land, and could not, therefore, be
removed out of it. Moreover, it was not removed to
Babylon, in any sense, literally or figuratively, and did
not remain there as the vision declares, (v. 11,) for the
Mohammedan occupants of that region are not idola-
ters. Hence the explanation that refers it to the entire
wickedness of the Jewish people of all kinds, is more
consistent with the preceding vision, and gives a better
sense. The mass of lead symbolizes the heavy judgment that God was holding over them, and which at the
fulness of time he would allow to fall. Accordingly,
the wicked woman is thrust down into the small measure, crushed and doubled together, and the heavy weight
laid upon her to keep her thus prostrate. Then there
appear two winged messengers, with outstretched pin-
ions, as if the wind was raising them up, and their

the ephah between the earth and the heaven.

10 Then said I to the angel that talked with me, Whither do these bear the ephah?

wings were strong for flight like those of the stork. There were two, because it required two persons to lift such a measure. They symbolized the messengers of God's wrath that should desolate Judea, and banish the people. They were to carry it into Shinar, which is here the symbol for an enemy's country, and not the exact country to which they were be exiled. There it was to be put in a house, shut up, and this house to be built strongly and securely for a permanent habitation, to show that this exile would not be like the first, a brief sojourn, but a long, weary and enduring banishment from the land of their fathers ; when their resting should not be on God, or on the rock Christ Jesus, but on "their own base," they should be left to themselves, weighed down like lead with judicial blindness, stupidity, darkness, and hardness of heart.

The vision then predicted what happened four hundred years afterwards, when the measure of their iniquity being full by the rejection and murder of the Messiah, their hearts being gross and their ears heavy, the hour of vengeance came. Then appeared the Roman eagles, and after the most desperate struggle, the Jewish nation was crushed, and scattered to the four winds, wandering in enemies' countries, not resting on the promise of God, but weighed down with leaden obstinacy, and resting on their own works and righteous-

11 And he said unto me, To build it shall be established, and set there it an house in the land of Shinar : and upon her own base.

ness. How striking the symbol! how fearful the ful-filment!

PRACTICAL INFERENCES.

(1.) Every individual, and every nation, has a measure of sin ; and until that measure is filled up, God's long-suffering will wait for repentance and reformation, (v. 5, 6.)

(2.) There hangs above each sinner a crushing weight of wrath, poised and ready to descend with overwhelm-ing destruction, (v. 7.)

(3.) If the measure is filled up, the weight shall fall and crush the sinner with its ponderous mass of punish-ment, (v. 8.)

(4.) The finally impenitent shall be driven from God into gloomy exile, and left to himself, "to rest on his own base," to be subject to the thrall of his own law-less lusts that he has so long pampered into strength, and to reap as he has sowed, through a long and limit-less banishment, (v. 11.)

1 And I turned, and lifted up mine eyes and looked, and behold, there came four chariots out from between two mountains; and the mountains *were* mountains of brass.

2 In the first chariot *were* red

VISION VIII.

CHAPTER 6 : 1—8.—*The Four Chariots.*

ANALYSIS.

I. The vision. Four chariots with four differently colored horses come forth from between two brazen mountains, (v. 1—4.)

II. The meaning of the vision: that they were God's agencies in executing his purposes of wrath and mercy on earth, (v. 5, 6.)

III. The result of these agencies, protection to the people of God, punishment to their enemies, (v. 7, 8.)

V. 1—8. "And I turned and lifted up mine eyes and saw, and behold four chariots came out from between two mountains, and the two mountains were mountains of brass. In the first chariot were red horses; and in the second chariot black horses; and in the third chariot white horses; and in the fourth chariot piebald and fleet (*or strong*) horses. And I answered and said unto the angel that talked with me, 'What are these, my lord?' And the angel answered and said unto me, 'These are the four winds of the heavens, going forth from standing before the Lord of the whole earth. That which has the black horses goes forth to the north country, and the white go forth following them; and the piebald go forth to the south country.' And the fleet went forth, and they desired to go that they might walk through the earth; and he said, 'Go walk through the earth;' and they walked through the earth! And he cried to me, and spake to me saying, 'Behold these that go forth into the land of the north have quieted my spirit in the land of the north.' "

THE scene of this vision is in all probability the valley of Jehoshaphat, which lies between Mount Moriah and the Mount of Olives. The reason for selecting this spot

horses; and in the second chariot
black horses;

3 And in the third chariot white

horses; and in the fourth chariot
grizzled and bay horses.

4 Then I answered and said unto

was its proximity to the temple, which was the standing
symbol of the theocracy. This was the nearest spot to
the temple, accessible to chariots, and hence the most
suitable for locating a vision which referred to the theocracy. The prophet saw four chariots coming forth
from between two mountains of brass. The chariot
being used mainly in war, and on great state occasions,
was a symbol of authority, and owing to its warlike use,
of judgment. The number four has the same significance here as in the four winds of Daniel, the four
cherubs of Ezekiel, the four angels at the four corners
of the earth in the Apocalypse, and the four horns and
four artificers of the second vision. Alluding to the
four points of the compass, it is the symbol of universality, a judgment that goes in every direction. The
two mountains were the mountains that stood around
Jerusalem, on one of which the temple stood. They
symbolized the immovable foundation on which the
theocracy rested, viz., the promise and purpose of God ;
and to give strength to this symbol, the mountains are
represented as brazen. Brass being a much more
valuable metal, both absolutely and relatively, to the
ancients than it is to the moderns, it serves to indicate
at once the strength of the protection with which God
surrounds the Church, like a mountain of brass, and the
resistless might that accompanied the judgment that was

the angel that talked with me, What   5 And the angel answered and said
are these, my lord?   unto me, These *are* the four spirits

thus threatened. The duality of the mountains is
probably not significant, or if so, has essentially the
same meaning with the two olive trees of vision fifth.
But it probably refers only to the locality of the temple,
which being on Moriah, a chariot could only approach
it by coming between two mountains. The chariots,
or winds, had been stationed at the temple, awaiting the
commands of God, and having received their commands the prophet sees them going forth to obey them.
The colors of the horses are significant. Red, the
color of blood indicates carnage ; black, sorrow and
death ; white, victory ; and piebald, a combination of
them all, with the additional epithet of strong or fleet,
to show the nature of the judgments to be inflicted.
The angel declares these chariots to be the four winds
of heaven, that are often in Scripture the symbols of
the means employed by God, to execute his will. Two
of the chariots go toward the north, the country of
Babylon ; one toward the south, Egypt, (these being
the two greatest enemies of Israel at that period ;) and
one, the red probably, here also called fleet, went
through all the earth, so as to include all possible enemies. More chariots are sent against Babylon than
Egypt because of her greater cruelty and guilt. The
black horses that went forth to Babylon, symbolized the
trouble that was coming upon that haughty city, and
the white horses that followed indicated that this trouble

of the heavens, which go forth from standing before the Lord of all the earth.

6 The black horses which *are* therein go forth into the north country ; and the white go forth after them ; and

would terminate in conquest and subjugation. This was fulfilled about three years after the utterance of the prophecy, when Babylon revolted against the Persian rule, and was completely destroyed by Darius. God explains the vision by declaring that the chariots that went forth against Babylon had appeased his wrath by inflicting punishment on that country, and it follows that the same is true of the other chariots, although the fact is not specifically mentioned. Babylon being the great enemy of the Jews, it only is mentioned, and others follow as a matter of course. For illustrations of the phrase, "quieted my spirit," in the sense of "pacify," see Ezek. 5 : 13 ; 16 : 41 ; 24 : 13.

Such is the vision. The general meaning of it is very clear. The enemies of the Church shall be punished, is the motto of the picture, and the purport of the vision. The immediate application of the truth was to the existing circumstances of the Jewish church, but it contains a general proposition or law of the divine procedure that is now in fulfilment, and will so continue until the restitution of all things spoken of by the holy prophets since the world began. Following the preceding vision, which denounced wrath on the Jews, it declares that after the Jews have been punished, God will destroy their enemies, who will also be the enemies of the Church. Now, as the threatened punishment of

the grizzled go forth towards the south
country.

7 And the bay went forth, and
sought to go that they might walk to

the Jews is not yet completed, so this punishment which was to follow that completion is also incomplete, and the main fulfilment yet to come.

We have therefore in this vision an instance of what has been called the continuous fulfilment of prophecy. This takes place when the prophecy is not so much a simple prediction of facts, as the annunciation of a great principle of divine procedure, in the garb of existing and well-known facts, but yet equally applicable to other facts all along the history of God's dealings with man. Thus the most abstract and formulated statement of the essence of this vision is, the enemies of the Church shall be punished. Its immediate application was to Babylon and Egypt, the existing representatives of the ancient enmity of the serpent's seed, but this application is of course but a single one, that does not exclude the future examples of this principle of the divine government, that may and must arise. This is wholly different from the old double sense of prophecy, and is a most obvious and reasonable canon of interpretation.

And how striking the fulfilment of this threatening, when we remember the circumstances under which it was made. Could the haughty nobles of Babylon, in the gorgeousness of its magnificence, and the pride of its power, have heard the threatening of this obscure Jew, amidst the ruins of Jerusalem, with what derision

and fro through the earth : and he
said, Get you hence, walk to and fro
through the earth. So they walked
to and fro through the earth.

and contempt would they have treated the threat! The
anathema that was so feebly uttered against the mightiest and richest city of the world, to the eye of sense
seemed like the ravings of lunacy. Yet that feeble
whisper was the uttered voice of Jehovah, and the
elements of ruin in their remotest lurking-place heard
the summons, and began to come forth. Slowly and
silently did they come up to this dread work, and yet
surely and resistlessly, until the glory of these high
palaces was dimmed, and the magnificence of these
gardens and temples was covered, and now the winds
whistle through the reeds of the Euphrates, where
Babylon then sat in her pride ; and loneliness, desolation and death are stationed there the sentinel witnesses of the truth that His word returns not to
him void, that His spirit is quieted in the land of the
north.

Egypt also was yet proud and powerful, Memphis
still sat in her queenly pride by the old and solemn
Nile, and Thebes still retained the glory of that wonderful architecture that yet amazes the world. They had
stood thus from the hoariest antiquity, and how should
it be thought that at the bidding of the descendant of
an Egyptian slave, this ancient magnificence would
depart. Yet this bidding was obeyed, and wave after
wave of desolation swept over this haughty land, until
now the pyramids, the sphinxes and the temples of the

8 Then cried he upon me, and spake unto me, saying, Behold, these that go toward the north country have quieted my spirit in the north country.

mighty past, but mock the degenerate baseness of the mournful present.

Thus was it later in history with Greece and Rome, thus shall it be with guilty and godless Europe, thus shall it be with every enemy of the Church, who attempts to thwart the designs of God in the world. But as the final development of this vision of judgment was to be subsequent to the completion of the threatened punishment of the Jews, we know that it has not yet received its last and mightiest fulfilment. That shall take place only when the Lord descends from heaven with a shout, with the voice of the archangel and the trump of God, and when he shall be revealed from heaven in flaming fire taking vengeance on all his enemies. Then, and not until then, shall this vision receive its last, its most terrible, and complete fulfilment, in the dread scenes of that day for which all other days were made.

PRACTICAL INFERENCES.

(1.) The history of the world is all arranged and conducted in reference to the destinies of the Church, and the agencies that control that history go forth from the seat of the Church's great head, the unseen temple, (v. 1.)

(2.) God has in operation every species of agency, human and angelic, animate and inanimate, needful for

9 ¶ And the word of the LORD came unto me, saying,

10 Take of *them of* the captivity, *even* of Heldai, of Tobijah, and of Jedaiah, which are come from Babylon, and come thou the same day, and go into the house of Josiah, the son of Zephaniah ;

the accomplishment of his purposes, and will send them forth at the proper time. Hence political changes and revolutions are, after all, only the moving of the shadow on the earthly dial-plate, that marks the mightier motions going forward in the heavens, (v. 2—8.)

VISION IX.

CHAPTER 6 : 9—15.—*The Crowning of Joshua.*

ANALYSIS.

I. The symbolic act. The prophet commanded to take of the silver and gold that a deputation from Babylon had brought, and make a crown to be placed on the head of Joshua, (v. 9—11.)

II. Its meaning. Joshua, the crowned high priest, typified the Messiah, who was to be at once priest and king, and who would complete the great work of redemption, and reconciliation between God and man, (v. 12—15.)

V. 9—15. "And the word of Jehovah came unto me saying: Take of (*them of*) the captivity, of Heldai, of Tobijah, of Jedaiah, and go thou in that day, and go to the house of Josiah the son of Zephaniah, who (*all*) have come from Babylon: and take thou silver and gold, and make crowns, and place them on the head of Joshua the son of Jozedek, the high priest. And speak to him saying, Thus saith Jehovah of Hosts: Behold a man whose name is BRANCH, from his place shall he grow up, and he shall build the temple of Jehovah. And he shall build the temple of Jehovah, and he shall bear majesty, and he sits and reigns upon his throne, and is a priest upon his throne, and the council of peace shall be between them both. And the crowns shall be to Helem and to Tobi-

11 Then take silver and gold, and   head of Joshua the son of Josedech,
make crowns, and set *them* upon the   the high priest ;

jah, and to Jedaiah, and to Hen the son of Zephaniah, for a memorial in the temple of Jehovah.   And the far off shall come and
build in the temple of Jehovah, and ye shall know that Jehovah
of Hosts hath sent me unto you, and it shall be thus (*to you*) if ye
will listen to the voice of Jehovah your God."

THIS vision concludes the revelations of that memorable night, and they end as they began, like other revelations of God, in Christ.   In this closing vision, or
rather living tableau, which he was commanded to have
made in concluding the visions of the night, two things
demand investigation : (1,) the symbolic action, and
(2,) the meaning of it, as explained by God himself.

(1.) *The symbolic action.*

A deputation of Jews had brought gold and silver
from Babylon to Jerusalem to aid in the erection of the
temple.   This deputation consisted of four men, who
represented those by whom they were sent.   This representative character appears in their names, which are
significant, and which, in two cases, are changed, to-call
attention as it would seem to their significant character.
Heldai, which means robust, is changed for Helem,
which means strong ; Tobijah means the goodness of
God ; Jedaiah is, God knows ; and Josiah, which signi-
fies God founds, is changed for the kindred name Hen,
grace, whilst the name of his father Zephaniah means
God protects.   In consequence of the peculiar grammatical construction of one clause, " who have come
from Babylon," it has been supposed that Josiah was

12 And speak unto him, saying, Thus speaketh the LORD of hosts, saying, Behold the man whose name *is* The BRANCH; and he shall grow up out of his place, and he shall build the temple of the LORD:

not of the deputation, but a resident of Jerusalem at whose house they lodged, and this would seem to have been the interpretation of our English translators, by their transposition of this clause to another part of the verse. But the position of it after the name of Josiah seems to be designed to indicate him as one of the number, and giving the relative ("who") its usual meaning, we have a clear and consistent sense. It is only necessary to suppose that Josiah was the treasurer of the deputation, and that the gold and silver were at his house, to see why it was necessary to go there to obtain it for this symbolic purpose. The prophet was commanded to take the other members of the deputation, and obtain from the whole of them a portion of the precious metals they had brought with them from Babylon. Of this metal he was to make crowns, or perhaps one crown compounded of two or more parts, such as Christ is represented as wearing, Rev. 19 : 12, (many crowns or diadems.) The verb is singular. This diadem, or combined crown, was to be placed on the head of Joshua the high priest, to set forth a great fact in the future, which is explained in the succeeding verses. The symbolic action then was, to take the gold and silver of the deputation, and make a crown which was first to be placed on the head of Joshua, and afterwards hung up as a memorial in the temple.

G

13 Even he shall build the temple of   and shall sit and rule upon his throne:
the Lord; and he shall bear the glory,   and he shall be a priest upon his

(2.) *The explanation of this symbolic action.*

There are two points involved in this explanation : 1st, what is meant by putting the crown on Joshua ; and 2d, why the material was taken from the treasure brought by the deputation.

1st. What did the crowning of Joshua signify ? Joshua, as high priest, we have seen in Vision IV., to be himself a typical person, and hence was fitted to receive this symbolic act, which was significant of an investiture with kingly authority. This kingly authority could not be promised to Joshua individually, for the office was limited to the family of David. It must then have referred to him in his typical character, as the representative type of the Messiah. This is put beyond doubt by the epithet Branch, which is really one of the appellations of the Messiah, as may be seen in Jer. 23 : 5, 33 : 15, and Zech. 3 : 8. Hence the crowning of Joshua was a typical representation of the conferring of kingly power on the Messiah.

We have in vs. 12, 13, a description of the Messiah. The phrase " from his place shall he grow up," is a description of his obscure origin. He shall not openly descend from heaven, in visible glory and greatness, but shall slowly grow up out of the earth, in lowly humiliation. This was true of him as a man, for he was the humble carpenter's son for thirty years, and grew slowly in the shade as a Nazarene. It was true of him as Mes-

throne : and the counsel of peace shall 14 And the crowns shall be to He-
be between them both. lem, and to Tobijah, and to Jedaiah,

siah, for he was a root out of a dry ground, despised
and rejected of man. It has been true of him as a
recognized Saviour in the world, for his Church began
as a little flock, and is yet in a minority among men.
It is true of him as a life in each heart, for Christ is
formed within us the hope of glory, gradually, first the
blade, then the stalk, and then the full ear in the stalk.
Hence this phrase is strikingly descriptive of the
Messiah as he has been actually manifested in the
person of Jesus.

The building of the temple of Jehovah, which is
repeated for emphasis, to show its prominence in his
work, is explained by Christ himself, when he says,
"destroy this temple, and in three days I will build
it again," which in like manner has its full significance
only in that Church which is at once the body of Christ,
and the spiritual temple founded on apostles and
prophets, with that corner-stone which the builders
rejected. "Bearing the majesty," refers to the kingly
glory that shall be his, in spite of his lowly origin. He
shall bear the crown. This is more fully expressed by
the words "he shall sit," (*i. e.* securely and permanently)
"reign," as a king, though the beginning of his kingdom
is thus obscure.

His character is more fully set forth in the next
phrase, "a priest upon his throne," which asserts the
kingly and priestly character of Messiah, as it is asserted

and to Hen the son of Zephaniah, for a memorial in the temple of the LORD.

15 And they *that are* far off shall come and build in the temple of the

in Ps. 110 : 4, " thou art a priest forever after the order of Melchisedek," *i. e.* a kingly priest, and a priestly king.

The phrase in v. 13, "the counsel of peace shall be between them both," refers to the union of the priestly and kingly offices in the work of redemption. " The counsel of peace " is the counsel that produces peace, and this is done by Christ in the exercise of these two offices, by one of which he purchases redemption, and by the other applies it ; by the one expiates sin, and by the other extirpates it ; and thus reconciling man and God, causes peace on earth, and good will to man. We have, then, in these words a full description of the atoning work of the Messiah, and the application of that work in the development of the Church.

We are now able to see, 2dly, why the material for the crown was taken from the gold brought by the deputation. It was to typify the introduction of the Gentiles into the Church. This is directly asserted in v. 15, " and the far off," (the very expression used by Paul in Eph. 2 : 17, to designate the Gentile Ephesians, "you that are afar off") shall come and build in the temple of Jehovah, and carry forward his glorious kingdom. This is then an exact parallel to ch. 2 : 11, 8 : 10, Isa. 60 : 9, 10, and many other passages of a like purport. The silver and gold were brought from the distant captives, and the crown was to be hung up

LORD ; and ye shall know that the
LORD of hosts hath sent me unto you.
And *this* shall come to pass, if ye will
diligently obey the voice of the LORD
your God.

in the temple as a memorial of the fact, that the distant
outcast nations were coming, and would one day be
admitted to the full privileges of the Church. The
condition of this blessing is then given in the words
that follow, declaring that if the theocratic people are
faithful they shall retain their privileges, but if unfaithful, they shall be cut off, and the wild olive branches
graffed into the original tree, and that the fulfilment of
this prophecy would prove his divine mission as a
prophet.

PRACTICAL INFERENCES.

(1.) We have here, then, a proclamation of the missionary character of the Church. Christ is yet a Branch,
yet growing, and not yet revealed, and hence men
reject him. But he is yet a king, despite of the lowliness of his Church, and the wickedness of men, and as
such we must acknowledge him. It is only by resting
upon him as a priest and as a king that our souls can
find peace. We must be pardoned by his atonement,
and governed by his laws, or we can never be at peace.
To those who refuse to receive him in these offices, he
will come again in power and great glory, to take vengeance on all his enemies, (v. 12, 13.)

(2.) The crown that yet hangs in the temple, is a call
to missionary activity. We may be able to do but
little, so were the Jews in Babylon, but that little must

be done, and God will bless us. We cannot go in person to this work, neither could they, but we may send our representatives as they did, to act in our place. Men are found willing to go far hence among the Gentiles, and only ask the Church to enable them to do so, and wo ! to the church that refuses to respond. Obedience is the condition of inheritance, and if we refuse to listen to God, God will refuse to listen to us, and will cast us off from his kingdom as he did the faithless Jews, and we remain as do they, a fearful memorial of the danger of neglecting the commands of God. How shall the far off hear without a preacher, and how shall they preach except they be sent. The missionary activity of the Church is the circulation of her life-blood ; suspend this and she swoons, stop it and she dies, (v. 14.)

(3.) The two great themes of the preacher are sin and salvation ; man a great sinner, Christ a great saviour ; and the great test of piety in preacher and people is the fervency of the missionary spirit, (v. 15.)

PART II.—DIDACTIC.

CHAPTERS 7, 8.

THE occasion that called forth this portion of the prophecy, was a question of casuistry. There was but one fast appointed by the Mosaic law, the day of atone-

ment, and this was rather an incident connected with
the day, than a prominent part of its observances. But
in process of time other stated fasts were instituted among
the Jewish people, which gradually became very strin-
gent in their binding authority. One of these was on
the anniversary of the capture of Jerusalem by Nebuchadnezzar, the 17th day of the 4th month ; or the
month Thammuz, answering to the moon of July. A
second was on the 9th day of the 5th month, Ab, (August,) commemorating the burning of the city by Nebu-
zaradan, and the destruction of the holy and beautiful
house of their fathers. A third was on the 3d day of
the 7th month, Tishri, (the moon of October,) in memory of the massacre of Gedaliah and others by Ishmael,
as recorded in Jer. 41 : 1—10. A fourth was on the
10th of the 10th month, Tebeth, (January,) the day
that Nebuchadnezzar commenced the siege of Jerusalem. These were all merely human appointments, but
like all similar additions to God's ordinances, they soon
obtain a control over the minds of the people that led
them into superstition. They were observed with great
care doubtless during the captivity, and even after the
return of the people from Babylon. But after the return, a question as to the propriety of their continuance arose in the minds of some, for the solution of
which they desired the declaration of the prophet.
Having been instituted on account of special reasons, the
query was, when the reasons are removed, shall the ob-

1 And it came to pass in the fourth year of king Darius, *that* the word of the LORD came unto Zechariah in the fourth *day* of the ninth month, *even* in Chisleu:

servances continue ? *cessante ratione, cessatne ipsa lex ?*— When the city is reinhabited, and the temple rebuilt, shall we continue to mourn statedly their destruction ? To answer these queries, a delegation was sent to the prophet, who, before replying to the direct question, reproves in ch. 7, the superstitions that had accumulated around the fasts, and then in ch. 8, answers the query in distinct and specific terms.

CHAPTER VII.

ANALYSIS.

I. A question about the propriety of continuing the stated fasts under the altered circumstances of the people, brings a delegation to the prophet to solve this doubt, (ch. 7: 1—3.)

II. The answer of the prophet.

(1.) A reproof of the selfish and godless motives that inspired their observances, (v. 4—7.)

(2.) An exhortation to the performance of weightier matters of the law, by the example of their ancestors, who, in spite of the warnings of the prophets to this effect, neglected these duties and were severely punished, (v. 8—14.)

(3.) A further exhortation to obedience by promises of the future prosperity of Jerusalem, (ch. 8 : v. 1—8.)

(4.) An exhortation to the vigorous prosecution of the erection of the temple by reason of the manifest favor of God already shown, and the fulfilment of the promises already made, (v. 9—12.)

2 When they had sent unto the house of God, Sherezer and Regem-me- lech, and their men and to pray before the LORD,

(5.) A further motive to obedience drawn from the future exten-sion of the theocratic blessings to the heathen, (v. 13—17.)

(6.) Having thus prepared their minds for the answer to the question about fasts, the prophet declares that they were all to be set aside as incongruous to the joyful condition of the theocra-cy, (v. 18, 19.)

(7.) He then concludes with a prediction of the calling of the Gentiles, of great dramatic beauty, thus linking the humble and struggling present with the magnificent and conquering future, and showing that all these passing duties of the present, were sig-nificant and important only because of their connection with the mightier unfoldings of the purposes of Jehovah in the scenes of the latter-day glory, (v. 20—23.)

The preliminary facts are stated in ch. 7 : 1—3.

V. 1—3. "And it was so in the fourth year of Darius the king, that the word of Jehovah was to Zechariah in the fourth. (*day*) of the ninth month, in Chisleu. And Bethel sent Sherezer and Regem Melech, and their men, to pray before the face of Jehovah; and to speak to the priests which were in the house of Jehovah of Hosts, and to the prophets, saying; Ought I to weep in the fifth month, separating myself, as I have done for so many years?"

The date of this transaction was two years after the symbolic visions of the preceding portion, and the tem-ple was therefore advanced near to its completion. The condition of the theocracy was prosperous and promis-ing, so that the people began to doubt the propri-ety of indulging mournful memories of the past, when

3 *And* to speak unto the priests
which *were* in the house of the LORD of

hosts, and to the prophets, saying,
Should I weep in the fifth month, sepa-

there was so much to excite joyful hopes of the future.

The only difficulty in these verses is in the second, where our version translates it, " when they had sent unto the house of God Sherezer," &c. This makes the singular verb (וִישְׁלַח) impersonal, and makes *Beth-el* an accusative, referring it to the temple. But the temple is never called *Beth-el*, but *Beth-Jehovah*, as in v. 3, and moreover the use of it in this clause would be rather tautological, as the latter part of the verse explains the where, and the why of this mission. Hence Maurer and Hengstenburg, following Lightfoot, refer *Beth-el* (the house of God) to the congregation, or the people of Israel. But this is equally unauthorized. There are instances of this tropical use of *beth*, referring to the people of Israel, but as far as we are aware of them, always in connection with Jehovah the covenant name of God, and never with El, which only expresses an attribute which belongs in smaller measure to creatures. *Beth-el* is uniformly used as the name of the old city of Luz, where the ark was for so long a time kept, and which for this reason was regarded as one of the sacred cities of the land. Usage, therefore, requires us to give it the same signification here, and the sense is a perfectly good one. The people of this old and sacred city would naturally be among the first to discuss such questions as these, and to send to Jerusalem for their solution.

rating myself, as I have done these so many years?

4 ¶ Then came the word of the LORD of hosts unto me, saying,

5 Speak unto all the people of the land, and to the priests, saying, When ye fasted and mourned in the fifth and seventh *month*, even those seventy

Hence it is said "Bethel sent," or the inhabitants of Bethel sent, &c., and in the reply it is intimated that the query was from a single city, for it is said, v. 5, "speak unto *all* the people of the land," as if to assure them that the reply was designed to have a scope wider than the source of the question. There is no reason for departing from the usual meaning of the terms. This is the view taken by Henderson, Ewald, Blayney, Hitzig, and the LXX. The fast of the 5th month is mentioned, because that was the commemoration of the destruction of the temple, an observance which would seem incongruous after the temple was rebuilt.

The deputation was sent first to pray, perhaps that God might solve their doubts, or bestow a fresh prosperity on Israel, and afterwards to seek at the mouth of his ministers the solution of their difficulties. The phrase rendered " pray," means to stroke the face, then to flatter by caressing, then to supplicate, or pray. (See Ex. 32 : 11 ; 1 Sam. 13 : 12.)

But the Jewish people needed something more than information in regard to the continuance of this fast. The whole doctrine of fasting had become overlaid with an incrustation of formalism and superstition, that needed to be broken up. Fasting had become not a means but an end, a mere form, as it is in Mohammedan and Papal countries at this day, and had attached to it an

years, did ye at all fast unto me, *even* to me?

6 And when ye did eat, and when ye

did drink, did not ye eat *for yourselves*, and drink *for yourselves?*

7 *Should ye* not *hear* the words which

opus operatum efficacy that wholly destroyed its real value.   They thought that God must bless them, indeed was bound to bless them, if they rigidly observed these outward rites, whatever was their inward character. Thus formalism in religion acted in the time of the restoration, precisely as it acted in every subsequent period in the history of the Church, leading men to be scrupulous about the mint, anise and cummin, the postures, costumes and rubrics of religion, whilst the weightier matters of justice toward man, and piety toward God, were neglected and forgotten.   Hence before a mere question of ritual observance could be settled, it was important that their minds should be set right on the deeper questions of their spiritual relations to God.   The prophet, then, instead of answering the question about the fast of the 5th month, proceeds to rebuke them for their selfish and stupid will-worship, and their ignorance in regard to the whole subject of fasting, not only as to this, but as to all the stated fasts that they had been observing.

V. 4—6. "Then was the word of Jehovah of Hosts to me, saying: Speak unto all the people of the land, and to the priests, saying, When ye fasted and mourned in the fifth and seventh month, these seventy years, did ye fast unto me, unto me?   And when ye ate, and when ye drank, was it not to yourselves that ye were eating, and to yourselves that ye were drinking?"

The grand error of all their observances, was that they were "without God;" not done because of his

the LORD hath cried by the former of round about her, when *men* inhabit-
prophets when Jerusalem was inhabited ed the south and the plain ?
and in prosperity, and the cities there-

command, not supported by his authority, not directed
to his glory, and not therefore deserving his approba-
tion.   The repetition of the phrase "unto me," at the
close of the 5th verse, is emphatic, and gives the key to
the passage.   Their fasting and feasting were alike selfish and godless, alike wanting in elevated aim, and alike
centered on themselves.   The radical principle of all
piety, reference to God, was wanting in all their conduct, and hence before asking questions about the form,
it were better to secure the substance ; before raising
questions about the outward manifestations of piety, it
were better to assure themselves that they have piety
itself.

But some might be disposed to plead ignorance as an
excuse.   The prophet meets this evasion by telling them
that this very ignorance was culpable in them, for they
had the teachings of the former prophets on this very
question of fasting.

V. 7. "Are not these the words which Jehovah cried by the
hand of the former prophets, when Jerusalem was inhabited and
in peace, and also her cities round about her, and when the south
and the plain was inhabited ?"

The English version makes "words" the object of a
verb understood, thus making the verse an expostula-
tion for disobedience, rather than an additional assevera-
tion.   But as the particle את is sometimes used to designate the subject of the verb, it is more natural to take

8 ¶ And the word of the LORD came unto Zechariah, saying,

9 Thus speaketh the LORD of hosts, saying, Execute true judgment, and shew mercy and compassions every man to his brother:

10 And oppress not the widow, nor the fatherless, the stranger, nor the poor; and let none of you imagine evil against his brother in your heart.

11 But they refused to hearken, and pulled away the shoulder, and stopped their ears, that they should not hear.

12 Yea, they made their hearts *as* an adamant stone, lest they should hear the law, and the words which the

it so here, thus obviating the necessity for an ellipsis. These are not novelties that are spoken in your ears, or words that have had no corroborating proofs. Are they not the very teachings of the older prophets? Did not Isaiah (ch. 58) and others assure you that it was not such a fast that God had chosen? Did they not warn your fathers, when all was yet prosperity, that such conduct would bring a curse on the land? And did not that curse descend and depopulate Jerusalem, and those regions round about her that once were crowded with life? Has not God then taught you alike by his word and his providence, and can you under such circumstances urge the plea of ignorance? If you follow your fathers in their sin, must you not also follow them in their suffering?

But that there might be no doubt in regard to the duties omitted, and the teachings neglected, the prophet gives an epitome of both in the following verses:

V. 8—10. "And the word of Jehovah was to Zechariah saying: Thus spake Jehovah of Hosts (*to your fathers*) saying: Judge the judgment of truth, and work kindness and compassion, every man toward his neighbor: and the widow, and the fatherless, the stranger and the poor, do not oppress, and do not devise evil in your hearts, any man against his neighbor."

These were the instructions given to their fathers by

LORD of hosts hath sent in his Spirit by the former prophets: therefore came a great wrath from the LORD of hosts.

13 Therefore it is come to pass, *that* as he cried, and they would not hear ;

so they cried, and I would not hear, saith the LORD of hosts:

14 But I scattered them with a whirlwind among all the nations whom they knew not. Thus the land was desolate after them, that no man

the former prophets ; but how these were received, and what were the consequences of this reception, are next pointed out.

V. 11—14. "But they (*your fathers*) refused to hear, and presented a refractory shoulder (*one that refused to wear the yoke*), and made heavy their ears against hearing : And their heart they made an adamant against hearing the law, and the words which Jehovah of Hosts did send in his spirit by the hand of the former prophets, wherefore there was great wrath from Jehovah of Hosts. And it came to pass, that as He cried and they did not hear, so they cry and I hear not, saith Jehovah of Hosts. And I scattered them to all nations whom they knew not, and the land was desolate after them, so that none went out or came in, and they made the land of desire to be desolate."

The meaning of these verses is very obvious. The disobedience of their fathers, and the punishment that followed, are held up to warn them against following in their footsteps. As they refused to wear the yoke of obedience, God laid upon them the yoke of oppression ; and as they hardened their hearts like the diamond against God's word, God broke these hard hearts by his judgments. When these judgments came down on them, they cried to God, but as they had refused to hear him, he then refused to hear them. The change of tense in v. 13, from the preterite in the first clause to the future in the second, is not accidental, but designed to show that the action is still continued,

passed through nor returned : for they laid the pleasant land desolate.

8 : 1 Again the word of the LORD of hosts came *to me*, saying,

2 Thus saith the LORD of hosts ; I was jealous for Zion with great jea-

lousy, and I was jealous for her with great fury.

3 Thus saith the LORD ; I am returned unto Zion, and will dwell in the midst of Jerusalem : and Jerusalem shall be called, A city of truth ;

which is the force of the Hebrew future in such a connection as this. (See Nordheimer's Grammar, § 967,1. a.) The meaning is that God had refused to hear their cry, and continued to do so even to the present time. Thus they had closed the throne of grace against themselves, and opened the throne of judgment. From this throne came forth the mandate of destruction, like a whirlwind, scattering them among their enemies, and leaving their pleasant land desolate, and desolate by their own wilful and persevering disobedience. The land of desire or delight was Canaan. (See Jer. 3 : 19.)

Having urged them to obedience by the fate of their fathers, the prophet next urged them by promises drawn from the future prosperity of Jerusalem, (ch. 8 : 1—8.)

V. 1—3. "And the word of Jehovah of Hosts was to me saying, Thus saith Jehovah of Hosts, I was jealous toward Zion with great jealousy, and with great fury was I jealous toward her. Thus saith Jehovah, I have returned to Zion, and I will dwell in the midst of Jerusalem, and Jerusalem shall be called 'city of the truth,' and the mountain of Jehovah, 'mountain of holiness.'"

The metaphor of the first verse is so common and obvious as to require no explanation, and yet it is full of instruction. God demands the whole heart, and will not be content with a divided throne. As the husband cannot brook the estrangement of his wife's affections to

and the mountain of the Lord of hosts,
The holy mountain.

4 Thus saith the Lord of hosts ;
There shall yet old men and old women dwell in the streets of Jerusalem,

and every man with his staff in his
hand for very age.

5 And the streets of the city shall
be full of boys and girls playing in
the streets thereof.

a rival, so God cannot allow the bestowal of our affections supremely to any other object. This is idolatry,
and as such will be punished with intense severity,
either in this world or in the next. But he assures
them, (v. 3,) that this outburst of anger is past, and that
now he has returned to Jerusalem with his former love,
and will dwell in her midst. God's presence in heaven
creates all its bliss, and God's presence on earth will
make it an antepast of heaven. But this will manifest
itself in an appropriate way. God is truth and holiness,
and they who enjoy his presence must partake of both.
Hence Jerusalem was to be a city of truth, and Moriah
a mountain of holiness. These phrases which are drawn
from Isaiah, are used in the same sense as in the older
prophet, and refer to the theocracy whose seat was in
Jerusalem, and therefore predict not simply the temporal enlargement of the nation, but the permanent
enlargement of the Church. This future prosperity is
further described in the next verses.

V. 4, 5. "Thus saith Jehovah of Hosts, there shall yet sit old
men and old women, in the streets of Jerusalem, and the man
whose staff is in his hand for multitude of days. And the streets
of the city shall be full of boys and girls, playing in the streets
of it."

The image here presented is one of great force and
beauty. The city rises before us as the glow of sunset

H

6 Thus saith the LORD of hosts; If it be marvellous in the eyes of the remnant of this people in these days, should it also be marvellous in mine eyes? saith the LORD of hosts.

begins to steal over Olivet, and the lengthening shadows begin to warn the laborer home. The streets are not silent or deserted, as they have hitherto been, but there sits the old man gazing on the scenes of peaceful beauty before him, while the aged companion of his earlier years sits by his side, to enjoy with him the freshening breeze that comes cool and sweet from the distant sea, while before them and around them are the merry shout, the joyous glee, and glad gambols of happy childhood, whose ringing echoes mingle sweetly with the tinkle of the bells and the lowing and bleating of the flocks that come softly from the hills as they hie them homeward to the nightly fold. There is an exquisite beauty in this picture that would strike a Jewish mind with peculiar force, to which the promise of old age and posterity was one of the richest that could be made. Indeed, the presence of the two extremes of life is one of the usual signs of prosperity. Old age and childhood not only grace a community, the one by its venerableness, and the other by its beauty, but they also prove its peace and prosperity. When war, famine, pestilence or anarchy, have been raging, there are but few of either class, for their feebleness makes them the earliest victims. Hence in the streets of Jerusalem, there were but few of either in her desolation, for even those who did remain abstained from coming forth from

7 Thus saith the LORD of hosts ; Behold, I will save my people from their houses through fear. But the time was coming the east country, and from the west country ;

their houses through fear.   But the time was coming when security would be so general, that old and young would meet in the peaceful streets without fear of molestation or injury.

In looking at the wider scope of this prediction, which sets forth the enlargement of the Church, although we may not say that it refers to the children of the Church whose connection with it has been sealed by the baptismal blessing, yet we will say, that no language could, with more significance and beauty, set forth this fact in the New Testament church, than this beautiful promise, of the children that shall be seen in the streets of the holy city.

But there seemed to be something almost incredible in these promises, and their faith was staggered by the very greatness of the blessing.   It is therefore added, to meet this feeling,

V. 6. "Thus saith Jehovah of Hosts, if it is wonderful in the eyes of the remnant of this people in these days, is it also wonderful in my eyes, saith Jehovah of Hosts ?"

The common error of men in regard to God, is judging of him by themselves.   Under the influence of this error, the Jews thought such promises incredible. But God assures them that they must not judge him by themselves, for though to their pusillanimous weakness it seemed a thing too wonderful for belief, yet it was not so to his mighty and unlimited strength.

8 And I will bring them, and they shall dwell in the midst of Jerusalem : and they shall be my people, and I will be their God, in truth and in righteousness.

9 ¶ Thus saith the LORD of hosts ;

V. 7, 8. "Thus saith Jehovah of Hosts, behold, I am he saving my people, from the land of the east, and from the land of the setting sun. And I will lead them, (viz. *from these lands to Jerusalem,*) and they shall dwell in the midst of Jerusalem, and they shall be my people, and I will be their God, in truth and righteousness."

The terms of this prediction carry us beyond any facts at that time existing, and refer to events then future. It predicts a return of the Jews from the west as well as the east, whilst at this time the only dispersion existing, was toward the east in Babylon. Hence, an universal dispersion is implied in this universal restoration, the terms, from east to west, being inclusive of the entire earth. This general dispersion did not occur until the final fall of Jerusalem, since which there has been no general restoration of the Jews, either in a literal or a figurative sense. Hence the main facts predicted, are yet future. That they include a literal restoration of the Jews to their own land is probable, but that this is the main purport of the prophecy, is just as improbable. There is something more than a mere political restoration required by the general drift of the prophecy, which is spiritual and not temporal, and which therefore demands a spiritual reunion to the spiritual theocracy, or the blood-bought and blood-washed Church of God. And this is particularly demanded by the covenant formula of v. 8, " they shall be my people, and I will be their God," which is always

Let your hands be strong, ye that hear in these days these words by the mouth of the prophets, which *were* in the day *that* the foundation of the house of the LORD of hosts was laid, that the temple might be built.

10 For before these days there was no hire for man, nor any hire for beast; neither *was there any* peace to him that went out or came in because of the affliction : for I set all men every one against his neighbor.

the exponent of spiritual blessings, and the fact is put beyond all question by the explanatory addendum, "in truth and righteousness," which expressly affirms that this restoration and union are not to be outward, visible and temporal, but inward, invisible and spiritual. They will be a sincere and justified people, as he will be a true and pardoning God. Hence, whilst the general sense of the prophecy has been fulfilled in every case wherein prosperity was bestowed on the Jewish nation before the advent of Christ, its terms have never been fully met by any event that has yet occurred, and we are to look for the grand restoration among those latter-day things that are to complete the restoration of all things spoken of by the holy prophets before the world began.

Having predicted this future prosperity to the theocracy, he uses this as a motive to urge them to the energetic prosecution of the rebuilding of the temple, (v. 9—12.)

V. 9, 10. "Thus saith Jehovah of Hosts, strengthen your hands, ye that in these days hear these words by the mouth of the (*some*) prophets who (*were*) in that day, when the house of Jehovah of Hosts was founded, that the temple might be built. For before these days there was no hire of a man, and hire of a beast, there was also none. And to him going out and coming in, (*the traveller*,) there was no peace from the enemy, and I stirred up all men, every man against his neighbor."

11 But now I *will* not *be* unto the residue of this people as in the former days, saith the LORD of hosts.

12 For the seed *shall be* prosperous; the vine shall give her fruit, and the ground shall give her increase, and the heavens shall give their dew; and I will cause the remnant of this people to possess all these *things*.

He urges them to carry forward the great work of the temple, as the proper mode of testifying their faith and hope in God, and enforces these urgencies by an appeal to their experience. The same prophets that promised prosperity at the foundation of the temple, (viz. himself and Haggai,) now promised yet greater prosperity if that temple was pushed on to final completion. He challenges an investigation into the truth of the predictions then given, and shows their fulfilment before their eyes. Then all was confusion, insecurity and trouble. Labor was not rewarded, for no man had the means of doing so, or the secure enjoyment of his property to induce him to employ either man or beast. Robbers and marauding parties of their enemies infested the country so much, that no man could travel through it without danger of becoming a victim. And to this external peril there was added internal strife, every man against his neighbor, so that all was anarchy and confusion. Such was the condition of affairs when the temple was founded, but as they prosecuted this work, prosperity and peace began to return, and now the whole aspect of things was changed, giving token that God had opened the windows of heaven and poured out upon them a blessing. Hence they had evidence before their eyes of the faithfulness of God to the words

13 And it shall come to pass, *that* as ye were a curse among the heathen, O house of Judah, and house of Israel ; so will I save you, and ye shall be a blessing ; fear not, *but* let your hands be strong.

of his holy prophets.   The continuance of this returning prosperity is then further promised.

V. 11, 12. "But now, not as in the former days, (*will*) I (*be*) to the remnant of this people, saith Jehovah of Hosts.   For the seed shall be safe, (*Heb. of peace,*) the vine shall give her fruit, and the earth shall give her produce, and the heavens shall give their dew, and I will cause the remnant of this people to inherit all these things."

The argument here is from the past to the future ; as God has fulfilled his promises heretofore, so will he hereafter.   Therefore go forward with this work.   And when we ascend from the temporary facts that called forth this appeal, to the more unchanging ones that are connected with them, we find the same principle to be true.   The faithfulness of God to his Church and people in the past, is a guarantee that he will not forsake them in the future, and an encouragement to go forward in the great work of erecting the spiritual temple, of which this material temple was but the outward symbol.   Let our hands be strong in this great work, by remembering the fact that God has ever been faithful to his promises in the past, and therefore will continue to be faithful to them in the future.

That the extended view we have taken of the prophecy is the true one, appears yet further from the next paragraph, in which the calling of the Gentiles is distinctly predicted, first implicitly and then explicitly.

V. 13. " And it shall be, that as ye have been a curse among the

14 For thus saith the LORD of hosts ; As I thought to punish you, when your fathers provoked me to wrath, saith the LORD of hosts, and I repented not:

15 So again have I thought in these days to do well unto Jerusalem and to the house of Judah : fear ye not.

16 ¶ These *are* the things that ye nations, oh house of Judah, and house of Israel, so I will save you, and ye shall be a blessing : fear not, (*therefore,*) strengthen your hands."

The words " curse " and " blessing," are here used, not in the sense of being a source of curse and blessing to the heathen, so much as an example of it so striking as to become proverbial. As the nations were accustomed to curse one another, by wishing that they might be as the Jews, so prostrate was their condition, so hereafter to wish this would be a form of benediction instead of malediction, so great would be their prosperity. For this concrete sense of these terms, see 2 Kings, 22 : 19 ; Jer. 24 : 9, and Gen. 12 : 2 ; Ps. 21 : 7.

V. 14—17. " For thus saith Jehovah of Hosts, as I determined to punish you (*the house of Israel*) when your fathers provoked me, saith Jehovah of Hosts, and I repented not, so, on the contrary, I have determined, in these days, to do good to Jerusalem, and to the house of Judah, fear not. These are the words which ye must do, (*obey,*) speak the truth, every man to his neighbor ; truth and the judgment of peace judge in your gates ; devise not evil in your hearts, each man against his neighbor, and an oath of falsehood do not love, for all these are the things which I hate, saith Jehovah."

The form of address in v. 14, furnishes an illustration of the organic unity in which the theocratic people were regarded by God. He says, "as I determined to punish *you,*" when the determination was really to punish their fathers, with whom they were, however, connected in this

shall do ; Speak ye every man the
truth to his neighbor; execute the
judgment of truth and peace in your
gates :

17 And let none of you imagine evil
in your hearts against his neighbor :
and love no false oath : for all these
are things that I hate, saith the LORD.

organic unity of the visible Church. A parallel but yet
more striking instance of the same thing, is found in
Haggai 2 : 5 : "According to the word which I cove-
nanted with *you* when ye came out of Egypt," where
the remoteness of date was so great, as to make
the form of expression possible only in view of this
federal unity, under the aspect of which, God delights
to contemplate his Church. Those who deride Abra-
hamic covenants, and covenant relations and blessings,
as mere sectarian figments, have with Esau's blindness,
though not, we trust, with Esau's guilt, undervalued
their birthright.

The argument is, that as the threatened punishment
has been so faithfully inflicted, so the promised blessing
will with equal fidelity be bestowed, and the argument
is *à fortiori*, if the work of severity, so alien to God's
character, has been inflicted with such inflexible determination, how much more shall that of goodness, which
is so much more consonant to his nature ?

The conditions of this promised blessing are set forth
in v. 16, 17, and the demonstrative "these" with which
the passage opens, indicates that a contrast is drawn
between these things, and the mere ritual and rubrical
questions that had engaged so much of their attention.
As if he had said, the question of humanly ordained
fasts is a very trifling one, for *these* are the weighty

18 ¶ And the word of the LORD of
hosts came unto me saying,

19 Thus saith the LORD of hosts;
The fast of the fourth *month*, and the

matters of the law, the observance of which is the great
duty of the people.   Do these things, and the minor
questions of ceremonies will soon be decided.   The sins
specified are those that it seems were most rife, falsehood, perjury, fraud, and injustice.   The expression
" in your gates," shows that the reference is to judicial
procedure, as the gate of the city was the place where
such business was transacted.   The reason given for
avoiding these sins, viz., because God hated them, is
instructive, for it brings out the great principle of piety
that runs through all revelation, that religion consists in
loving what God loves, and in hating what God hates,
our nature being thus brought into conformity with His.
When this is done, the creature has reached the completeness of its development, and hence this is the grand
rule of conduct and attainment.

The prophet now at length proceeds to answer the
question about fasts, and answers it more fully than it
had been asked.   The query was only in regard to a
single fast, that which commemorated the burning of
the city and temple, but the prophet adduces all the
fasts, and gives the same rules regarding them all.
They were all to be turned into days of rejoicing.

V. 18, 19. " And the word of Jehovah of Hosts was to me, saying, ' Thus saith Jehovah of Hosts, The fast of the fourth (*month*,)
and the fast of the fifth, and the fast of the seventh, and the fast
of the tenth, shall be to the house of Judah for joy and gladness,
and for festal observances, therefore love the truth and peace.' "

fast of the fifth, and the fast of the
seventh, and the fast of the tenth,
shall be to the house of Judah joy and
gladness, and cheerful feasts ; therefore love the truth and peace.

For the fast of the fourth month (Thammuz 17th),
in which Jerusalem was captured, see Jer. 52 : 6, 7 ;
for that of the fifth month (Ab. 9th), see 2 Kings 25 :
8 ; for that of the seventh month (Tishri 3d), for the
massacre of Gedaliah see Jer. 41 : 1—10 ; and for that
of the tenth month (Tebeth 10th), the beginning of the
siege of Jerusalem, see 2 Kings 25 : 1, and Jer. 52 : 4.
So far from the continuance of these days of fasting,
they were to be changed into days of festivity, so great
would be the blessing on the people. When God
makes the sun shine, the tear-drops should be dried ;
and when his blessing comes upon us, the memory of
our sorrows should be used only to enhance our present
joy. But the moral condition of this is reiterated,
" love truth and peace." God will bless, but not in
spite of man's wickedness.

The ground of this joy is then more fully set forth,
and shown to be the conversion of the Gentiles, or the
enlargement of the Church from its narrow Jewish form
to its wide and comprehensive universality in the Messianic period.

V. 20—23. " Thus saith Jehovah of hosts, It shall yet be that
peoples shall come, and the inhabitants of many cities. And they
shall go, the inhabitants of one (city) to another, saying, ' Let us
go to pray before Jehovah and to seek Jehovah of Hosts.' ' I
will go also.' And they shall come, many peoples and many nations, to seek Jehovah of Hosts in Jerusalem, and to pray before
Jehovah. Thus saith Jehovah of Hosts, In those days (it shall be)

20 Thus saith the LORD of hosts; come people, and the inhabitants of
It shall yet *come to pass*, that there shall many cities:

that they shall seize (*viz. :*) ten men from all the tongues of the
nations, they shall seize the skirt of a man (*that is*) a Jew, saying,
'We will go with you, for we have heard that God is with you.'"

The form of this prophecy is highly dramatic. The
scope of it is to predict the introduction of the Gentiles
into the theocracy, and the consequent enlargement of
the Church. This is described by a bold and beautiful
personification. A movement is seen among the nations
that have hitherto hated the Jews, a pervading and
powerful movement, that stirs them to their remotest
extent. The inhabitants of one city run to another in
their eagerness, and cry, "let us go to pray before Jehovah, &c." The instant response of each one thus
addressed is, "I will go also." The intensity of the
feeling is set forth partly by the abruptness of the
expressions, and partly by the intensive verbal form in
the Hebrew, "let us go, going," *i. e.* let us all certainly
and speedily go, lest we be too late. Thus they start,
not by ones and twos, but in crowds to hasten to Jerusalem, that they may secure the favor of God. As they
near the holy city, they run to seize the outer garment
of a Jew, ten of the crowding Gentiles eagerly sur-
rounding one of the Jews, to cast in their lot with
them, to become one of their number, and to share
their privileges because they have heard that God is
with them. The numbers ten and one are used in that
definite for an indefinite sense, which we have in

21 And the inhabitants of one *city* shall go to another, saying, Let us go speedily to pray before the LORD, and to seek the LORD of hosts : I will go also.

22 Yea, many people and strong na-

English in the expression "ten to one," and which is common in the Bible, see Gen. 31 : 7; Lev. 26 : 26, &c. The phrase "from all the tongues of the nations," is of course an easily understood idiom for nations using all the different languages. To seize the hem of the garment is a gesture of earnestness, importunity, and perseverance, which is emphatic were it done by only a single person, but when done by ten persons, it becomes significant of an intensity of anxiety, and a depth of conviction, of the very highest grade.

When this prediction was uttered nothing seemed more hopelessly improbable than its fulfilment. The Jews were a poor, despised, obscure tribe in the heart of Syria, whose existence was only known to the mighty world by their furnishing a trophy to the victorious arms of Babylon. Greece was just rising in the firmament of human history, and as she ascended to her brilliant zenith, her track was marked by the sweeping of the phalanxes of Alexander and the legions of Antiochus over the hills and valleys of Judea. And yet this prophecy remained unfulfilled. Rome was then in the rugged feebleness of her wolf-nursed infancy, and slowly continued to grow until she reached that gigantic stature in which she ruled the earth, and her conquering legions under Pompey again swept over this fated land, and even desecrated the places of her holy solem-

tions shall come to seek the LORD of hosts in Jerusalem, and to pray before the LORD.

23 Thus saith the LORD of hosts; In those days *it shall come to pass*, that ten men shall take hold, out of all lan-

nities. Five hundred years rolled away, and yet this prophecy remained unfulfilled, indeed seemed further from fulfilment than when it was uttered.

But at length the time arrived, and there came to Jerusalem " men out of every nation under heaven— Parthians, Medes and Elamites, and the dwellers in Mesopotamia, and in Judea and Cappadocia, in Pontus and Asia, Phrygia and Pamphylia, in Egypt, and in the parts of Lybia about Cyrene, and strangers of Rome, Jews and proselytes, Cretes and Arabians," all came up to Jerusalem to seek the face of Jehovah, and from the lips of a Jew they heard words that caused them to cry out " Men and brethren what shall I do ?"   They scattered to their own homes again, and carried with them the strange words that had so deeply moved their souls, and being followed by these wonder-working men, there soon began to work a new life among the nations of the earth, and this life took hold in its origin and efficacy upon *a Jew*.   Greece with her polished dialectics, Rome with her mailed mightiness, Asia with her soft voluptuousness, all submitted to the authority of a Saviour who was a Jew ; all rested their hopes for eternity upon a Jew ; and soon received as divinely inspired the words and writings of men who were Jews.   And for nearly two thousand years the mightiest intellects and largest hearts of the race, have breathed the spirit

guages of the nations, even shall take
hold of the skirt of him that is a Jew,
saying, We will go with you : for we
have heard *that* God *is* with you.

and studied the words of men who were Jews, and
have sought as the most precious boon of existence the
privilege of being covered with a robe of righteousness
that was wrought by the divinely incarnated hands of
one who is of the seed of Abraham after the flesh,
though as to his higher nature, God over all blessed
forever.　And at this day there are literally men of all
nations, and kindreds, and tribes, and people, who are
laying hold of the skirt of him that is a Jew, and cast-
ing in their lot with those whom God chose to be a
people for himself, and resting their hopes on that crucified Jew, who is the Saviour of the world.　Hence
thus far, the prophecy has been amply fulfilled, but its
grandest fulfilment is yet to come when Jerusalem shall
arise from the dust of her degradation, and Moriah be
crowned with the symbols of a pure worship, and Olivet
echo to the songs of the ransomed of Zion who shall
return with joy and everlasting gladness.　Then and
not until then shall this prophecy have its grandest and
fullest fulfilment, in the glory of the latter-day restoration of Israel.

　　And it is beautiful to remark the diffusive missionary
spirit that must accompany this great enlargement to
Israel, showing as it does the identity of all true religion.
The inhabitants of one city shall not be content with
idly waiting until another city shall hear of these glad
tidings, nor shall they merely send by another, but they

shall *go*, and themselves urge this great duty of seeking the Lord, and urge by the powerful suasion of example. " Let *us go*," with its loving earnestness shall then meet with the glad response, " I will go also."   And as clouds and doves to their windows shall they come, and lay hold, by a faith that will take no denial, of him who is the only name under heaven by which men can be saved. Thus the kingdom of heaven shall suffer violence, and the violent shall take it by storm.   How beautifully all this comports with the religion of the New Testament in its living and glowing form, we need not point out ; and how exactly the teachings of the prophet in regard to fasts and external ceremonies correspond with the teachings of Christ and Paul, we need not unfold at length, but only refer the thoughtful reader to their coincidences, as instructive proofs that after all, the Religion of the Bible is the same, by whomsoever taught, and the Old and New Testament but different stages in the growth of the same great tree of life, whose leaves are for the healing of the nations.   May every Christian resort to its balm-breathing leaves more constantly and earnestly, and he shall find them ever rich with angels' food that shall give his soul her daily bread.

PRACTICAL INFERENCES.

Many of these have been anticipated, but a few others may be briefly enumerated.

(1.) Prayer ought to precede every undertaking, but especially every religious undertaking, (7 : 1, 2.)

(2.) When we are in doubt as to any case of duty, we should spread it before the Lord. When the fire descends from heaven on the altar, its light will enable us to see clearly, (v. 3.)

(3.) All stated fasts tend to degenerate into superstition, unless there is some strong counteracting agency. The original reference to God is lost in the mere outward act. This is the case with the Popish observances of the present day, (v. 5.)

(4.) Selfishness is the bane of all true piety, as godliness is its essence, (v. 6.)

(5.) Warnings of punishment when no signs of it are seen, are too often disregarded, (v. 7.)

(6.) They who cherish hard hearts, must expect hard treatment. The harder the stone, the harder will be the blow of the hammer to break it, (v. 8—14.)

(7.) They who will not bear the burden of obedience, must bear the burden of punishment, (v. 11.)

(8.) Loving anything as much as God, is unfaithfulness to his love, (c. 8 : 1.)

(9.) Men judge God by themselves in interpreting his promises, much oftener than in interpreting his threatenings, (v. 2.)

(10.) God does not forget his threatenings any more than his promises, (v. 14, 15.)

(11.) When God covenants with his people, he also covenants with their children, (v. 17.)

(12.) All true piety is instinct with the missionary spirit, desire for the salvation of others, (v. 20—23.)

I

Part IV.—Prophetical.

Chapter 9—end.

THE first question that meets us in regard to this portion of Zechariah, is its authenticity, or, whether it is the production of Zechariah. It is plain that this is a question totally distinct from its inspiration. It may be a part of the word of God, and yet wrongly ascribed to Zechariah. This question is still strongly discussed by able critics on both sides, and therefore cannot properly be passed by in an attempt to elucidate the prophecy.

One of the first to question its authenticity was Joseph Mede, who, in his remarks on Matthew 27 : 9, 10, Epist. 31, says : " It may seem the Evangelist would inform us that those latter chapters ascribed to Zachary (namely, 9th, 10th, 11th) are indeed the prophecies of Jeremy ; and that the Jews had not rightly attributed them. Certainly, if a man weigh the contents of some of them, they should in likelihood be of an elder date than the time of Zachary ; namely, before the captivity, for the subjects of some of them were scarce in being after that time. And the chapter out of which St. Matthew quotes (c. 11), may seem to have somewhat much unsuitable with Zachary's time ; as a prophecy of the destruction of the temple, then when he was to encourage them to build it. And how doth the sixth verse of that chapter suit with his time ? There is no Scripture saith they are Zachary's, but there is Scripture saith they are Jeremy's, as this of the Evangelist. As for their being joined to the prophecies of Zachary, that proves no more they are his than the like adjoining of Agur's proverbs to Solomon's proves they are therefore Solomon's, or that all the Psalms are David's, because joined in one volume with "David's Psalms." Mede was followed in this opinion by Hammond, Kidder, Bridge, Whiston, New-come and Secker, among the English commentators. On the continent this view was adopted by Flügge, Döderlein, J. D. Michaelis, Seiler, Eichhorn, Bauer, Bertholdt, Forberg, Rosenmüller, Corrodi, Gramburg, Hitzig, Credner, Maurer, Ewald and Knoble. J. Pye Smith and Davidson, in England, also take this side of the question. De Wette, in the earlier editions of his *Einleitung*, took this position, but in the later editions avows his belief that they were written by Zechariah. The authorship of Zechariah has been defended by Blayney, Carpzov, Beckhaus, Jahn, Koester, Hengsten-berg, and Burger. It will thus be seen that there is much weight of authority on both sides. Among those who deny the authorship of Zechariah, there is great diversity of opinion as to the real authorship. Mede ascribes them to Jeremiah, and supposes that his pro-phecies were in a fragmentary and confused state during the captivity, and were arranged by Zechariah. Eichhorn refers one part to the time of Alexander ; Corrodi, the 14th chapter to the time of Antiochus

Epiphanes ; Bertholdt, a part to an author in Josiah's time, and a part later ; Rosenmüller, to the age of Uzziah ; and indeed each critic has his own peculiar theory as to the date and the authorship of these chapters. This great variety of view shows that the marks of date are by no means so clear as those affirm who deny the authenticity ; for if they were, there would be more uniformity. Hence, we are led to look at the reasons for this denial more carefully.

(1.) The first reason adduced by Mede is the ascription of the passage in Zech. 11 : 12, 13, to Jeremiah, by Matthew. This is the only point about which there is any real difficulty. We cannot, with the neologist, say that it was a slip of memory on the part of the Evangelist, for this would be to deny his plenary inspiration. Nor can we suppose with some that the Evangelist quotes from an apocryphal book ascribed to Jeremiah. There was such a book, as we learn from Jerome ; but it was obviously, as he pronounced it, a spurious fabrication of a later age than that of the apostles. Henderson, Griesbach, and others, suppose that there has been an error of the copyist. They, believing the gospel of Matthew was written in Hebrew, show how such an error might readily be made. But this hypothesis in regard to the original language of this gospel is not sufficiently proved to make it the basis for another hypothesis. Others conjecture that 'Ιριου was written by some early copyist instead of Zριου. This last supposition is by no means improbable. Dr. Henderson cites a number of MSS., in which the name Jeremiah is omitted, or that of Zechariah inserted.. But after all, the weight of authority yet is in favor of the common reading, and hence we must look for some other explanation. The one which, on the whole, seems to be most reasonable, is that of Hengstenberg, that the Evangelist quoted the earlier prophet on whose prophecy the later one was based, to indicate this connection. The reasons on which this view is based, may be seen drawn out more fully in the notes on Chapter 11: 12, 13, and need not here be repeated. One thing is very certain, that in the age of the apostles this portion of the prophecy was ascribed to Zechariah, for it occupies that place in the LXX., which was written three hundred years before, and used by our Lord and the writers of the New Testament. It does not seem probable that the Evangelist would make a correction of the Jewish Canon, in this indirect manner, without giving some intimation to that effect. The uniform reference of these chapters to Zechariah in the Jewish Canon, is much more difficult to account for, if he did not write them, than the verse in Matthew is, if he did. Hence we are led to the conclusion that this reference was not intended to deny the received opinion that these chapters were a part of the prophecies of Zechariah, and rightly referred to him as their author.

(2.) It is said that the contents refer it to an earlier age than that of Zechariah. This depends on the interpretation of particular passages which it will after-

wards be seen do not require this interpretation.
Ephraim is mentioned, but it is used as it is in the prophetic writings, as the designation of Israel, and we
find Israel spoken of in Malachi in a manner precisely
similar, and yet no one from this fact infers that
Malachi lived before the captivity. There is not the
slightest intimation that there was a separate political
organization in Israel at the time when the prophecy
was written.

Other texts will be found to refer to events after the
time of Zechariah, and not before, as we examine them
in detail. The absence of all references to a King as
existing in Judah or Israel, clearly intimates that the
prophecy was written at a time when the kingly office
had ceased to exist. This fact has led Eichhorn and
others to place the date of these chapters as late as the
age of Alexander.

(3.) It is alleged that a prophecy of the destruction
of the temple would have been most unlikely in Zechariah, whose object was to urge its erection. This would
be true if the prophecies were uttered at the time of
its erection. But they were probably uttered toward
the close of the prophet's life, and many years after the
temple was completed. Hence this objection rests on a
confusion of dates.

(4.) The difference of style is also alleged. This is
accounted for in part by the difference of age, the early
portions being written when the prophet was a young
man (ch. 2 : 4), and in part by the difference of aim

in the prophecy. Differences just as great appear in other prophecies whose authenticity has never been questioned. In Amos the first two chapters have one style and one formula of address, "Thus saith Jehovah;" the next three another, "Hear ye this word;" and the seventh and eighth a third, "Thus hath Jehovah showed me." But no critic has thought of dismembering Amos on this account. And yet the differences in this prophecy are not more important or decisive of a different hand. The purposes for which the three portions of Zechariah were written were so different that they demanded a difference of style fully as great as we actually find. To refer these portions to different authors would be as valid a procedure in criticism as to say that the author of the Treatise on the Sublime and Beautiful could not be the author of Reflections on the French Revolution, or that the author of Paradise Lost could never have written Paradise Regained, or the Doctrine and Discipline of Divorce. There is no difference of style or expression that is not fully accounted for by the interval that probably elapsed between the composition of the first and third portions, and the different purposes they had in view.

Hence, in view of the facts that these chapters were ascribed to Zechariah by those who formed the Jewish Canon, under divine guidance, as we believe, and but a few years at most after the death of Zechariah; that they were so regarded when the Septuagint translation was made three hundred years before the time of our Lord and the apostles ; that this opinion was unchallenged by any inspired writer, with an ambiguous exception, which is susceptible of another interpretation ; that the contents of these chapters have nothing that refers them to any other age, except we deny the possibility of prophecy, with the neologists; and that the reason obviously animating many of the assailants of the authenticity, is a desire to disprove their prophetic character, we feel constrained to adhere to the general judgment of both the Jewish and Christian churches, that these chapters belong to the prophecies of Zechariah, and are so to be interpreted.

The contents of this portion of the prophecy are of great variety, and intended obviously for the whole Church, stretching as they do from the time of the prophet to the undeveloped future when Christ shall return a second time without sin to salvation. This will be seen by an enumeration of the various discourses. I. The Syrian conquests of Alexander, c. 9 : 1—8. II. The lowly King Messiah, v. 9—12. III. The Maccabean deliverance, v. 11—17. IV. Future blessings to Judah, c. 10 : 1—5. V. The restoration of the Jews, v. 6—12. VI. The storm preceding the coming of Christ, c. 11 : 1—3. VII. Christ assuming the pastoral care of the Theocratic people, v. 4—14. VIII. The curse of evil rulers after the rejection of Christ, v. 15—end. IX. Future blessings to Judah, c. 12 : 1—9. X. Future repentance and blessing to Jerusalem, v. 10—end. XI. Fruits of penitence, c. 13 : 1—6. XII. The sword awaking against the shepherd, v. 7—9.   XIII. Future glories of the Church, chap. 14.

It will be seen at a glance that these prophecies carry us to some of the deepest soundings of the vast ocean of prophetic revelation ; and if the chart we shall present of this portion of it should not be satisfactory to all, they who have fathomed these depths lowest will be best prepared to make allowance for any failures.

I. THE SYRIAN CONQUEST OF ALEXANDER.

CHAPTER 9 : 1—8.

ANALYSIS.

I. The threatening, and the reason for it, (v. 1.)

II. The course of conquest traced, beginning at Damascus and extending along the Mediterranean coast to the Philistine cities, (v. 2—7.)

III. The safety of the Jewish people amidst these conquests of Alexander.

V. 1. " A BURDEN, the word of Jehovah on the land of Hadrach, and Damascus shall be its rest, for to Jehovah is the sight of man, and all the tribes of Israel."

V. 1. THIS prophecy most obviously predicts the conquests of Alexander the Great in the countries that bordered the Holy Land.   Its introduction here is appropriate, because it refers to a state of facts that would affect the Theocracy, and would also, at the same time, affect the enemies of Israel.

The word " burden" seems to be a sort of title or

1 The burden of the word of the
LORD in the land of Hadrach, and
Damascus *shall be* the rest thereof :
when the eyes of man, as of all the

motto to the prophecy to indicate its minatory character. It is never prefixed to prophecies of any other
character, and seems to be an appropriate inscription
to such predictions, that hang in the Bible, like dark
clouds, surcharged with a burden of wrath. The metaphor is so natural and common, that it is wonderful
that any attempt should be made to deny the obvious
significance of this word as marking those utterances
of prophetic inspiration that contain heavy tidings.
The elaborate investigation of Hengstenberg has so
completely established this meaning of the word that it
may be considered as settled.

The name Hadrach is somewhat obscure. Hengstenberg considers it a symbolical name for Persia,
compounded of terms signifying "strong—weak," but
his reasoning is too fanciful to be admitted. As all the
other names are actual names of cities, we would not
expect a symbolical name without some reason that
does not appear in the passage. Others say that there
was a city of this name near Damascus, but it is very
doubtful whether such a city ever existed ; and if it did,
whether its importance was such as to justify its place
at the head of this prophecy. Hence the opinion of
Henderson is the most probable, that it is the name of
a king, and perhaps a corruption of the common name
of the kings of Syria, Hadad. Whatever view be
taken, the general meaning of the prophecy is the

tribes of Israel, *shall be* towards the
LORD.

2 And Hamath also shall border

thereby: Tyrus, and Zidon, though
it be very wise.

same. The tempest was first to fall on this land, whatever it was.

"And Damascus shall be its rest." This is a parallel
passage to ch. 6 : 8, where it is said that the anger of
the Lord shall rest on the north country. The meaning is that a permanent judgment shall rest on Damascus, implying that this judgment should not be of a
wholly destructive character, and hence Damascus remains until the present day.

The next clause assigns the reason for these judgments, and hence begins with the particle "for." The
common interpretation of the phrase, "to Jehovah is
the eye of man," makes it an expression of the providence of God ; but if "eye" retains its ordinary signification, it should be in construction with Jehovah and
not with man, to express the fact that the oversight of
Jehovah was directed to man, and the sentence should
read "to man is the eye of Jehovah." Kimchi, Calvin, Blayney, and Henderson take the words in their
natural order, and make the clause mean that men and
the tribes of Israel look to God in this time of trouble.
They take כִּי as a particle of time. But this view does
not cohere with the context fully, which seems to require a reason for the infliction of the judgment rather
than the looking of men to God under it. This will be
done if we give to עַיִן the sense of *adspectus* or *appear-*

3 And Tyrus did build herself a the dust, and fine gold as the mire of
strong hold, and heaped up silver as the streets.

ance, a sense that it has in several passages. (See
Num. 11 : 7 ; Ez. 1 : 4 ; Dan. 10 : 6, &c.) The meaning then would be that the relative aspects of the world
and the people of Israel had come up before God, he
had seen their situation, and hence would bring judgments upon the one whilst he protected the other. The
general idea is clear, that these judgments are brought
upon the lands in question because the attention of
God was directed to them, as well as to the tribes of
Israel, and would equalize any apparent anomalies in
their relative conditions.

V. 2. "Also Hamath shall border on it, Tyre and Sidon because
it is very wise."

Hamath, which lay at the entrance to Palestine from
Damascus, should not only border on Damascus in ter-
ritory, but also in treatment, and should lie in the track
of the conquering invader. Pursuing his southern
course he should reach Tyre and Sidon, whose conceit
of wisdom and godless pride must be punished. The
Tyrians were celebrated for their worldly wisdom.
(See Ezek. 28 : 3—5, 12, 17.) When Alexander desired admission to their city under the pretext of sacri-
ficing to Hercules, they replied that the ancient and
true temple of that god was at Old Tyre, on the main
land, and sent him a crown of gold to conciliate him,
and prevent him from urging an entrance into their
city.

4 Behold, the Lord will cast her   the sea ; and she shall be devoured
out, and he will smite her power in   with fire.

Tyre and Sidon were two of the oldest and richest
cities in the world, the one famed for her arts and man-
ufactures, especially in glass and pottery, the other for
her commerce. The fine harbor of Tyre had made her
the depôt for the rich stream of Asiatic trade whose
current has always enriched the channels through which
it flowed, and her merchant princes were among the
rulers of the world. Having almost a monopoly of the
carrying trade of the Mediterranean, her wealth became enormous, and her inhabitants lived in a style of
luxury that has but few parallels in history. Like
Venice in modern times, she became arrogant and con-
temptuous in her feelings towards other nations, and
especially towards the Hebrews, because of their com-
parative poverty. Hence that offensive pride alluded
to in this verse.

V. 3. "And Tyre has built for herself a strong hold, and has
heaped up silver as dust, and gold as the mire of the streets."

Old Tyre had been built on the continent, but owing
to its greater exposure to invasion, another city was
erected on an island about half a mile from the shore.
The prophecies of Isaiah and Ezekiel seem to have
been directed against Old Tyre, and were fulfilled to
the letter by Nebuchadnezzar, who razed the city to its
very foundations and left it a heap of ruins. After the
overthrow of Old Tyre, the Tyrians concentrated their
strength on the island, surrounded it with a double wall

5 Ashkelon shall see *it*, and fear ; rowful, and Ekron : for her expecta-
Gaza also *shall see it*, and be very sor- tion shall be ashamed ; and the king

150 feet high, filled in with 25 feet of earth, which together with the surrounding sea, made the city apparently impregnable.   This is the " strong hold" mentioned by the prophet, and her flourishing commerce had at this time made silver and gold to be heaped up in her coffers like the dust of the streets. For the prophet to predict her overthrow, would be like a modern seer to predict the razing of Gibraltar or the sacking of London.   Yet it was precisely then that he declared that this proud queen of the waters should be overthrown.

V. 4. " Behold the Lord will dispossess her, and will cast into the sea her bulwark, and she shall be consumed with fire."

It is here predicted that the Lord would dispossess her from her strong seat, cast her girdling bulwark into the sea, and that she should be consumed with fire. Two hundred years passed away, and still Tyre sat in her queenly pride on the throne of the seas, and no power on earth seemed likely to attempt the fulfilment of this prophecy. At length there appeared on the shore an army of Greeks, who demanded the surrender of the city. But they were without a navy, and without any means even of reaching these mighty walls, or arresting for a moment the commerce that thronged her ports, and we cannot wonder that the Tyrians derided the presumption of the young chieftain. But her hour was come. Alexander, after various expedients, finally re-

shall perish from Gaza, and Ashkelon shall not be inhabited.

6 And a bastard shall dwell in Ash-

dod, and I will cut off the pride of the Philistines.

solved to take the ruins of Old Tyre, and run a mole from the shore to the island, which, after incredible labor he did, thus fulfilling another prophecy, that the very dust of Old Tyre should be scraped off, and her stones, timber and dust be laid in the midst of the water! (See Ezek. 26 : 4—12, &c.) Having completed this mole, he took the city after a siege of seven months, put to the sword about 10,000, enslaved 30,000, and burnt the city with fire, thus, against the most stupendous improbabilities, fulfilling this remarkable prophecy to the very letter.

V. 5, 6. "Ashkelon shall see it and fear, Gaza (*shall see it*) and tremble greatly, and Ekron, for her reliance is disgraced, and a king shall perish from Gaza, and Ashkelon shall not be inhabited. An alien shall dwell in Ashdod, and I will destroy the pride of the Philistines."

These verses describe the conquering march of Alexander along the shore, and depict the terror that the Philistian cities felt when they heard that even Tyre (which is called the reliance of Ekron, that being the most northern city of the Philistines, and nearest to Tyre) had been overthrown. This we know from history to have been the precise track of Alexander; and so completely have these prophecies been fulfilled, that the traveller can hardly discover the sites of some of these once proud and powerful cities. The perishing of a king from Gaza, is the destruction of her form of

7 And I will take away his blood out of his mouth, and his abominations from between his teeth ; but he that remaineth, even he, *shall be* for our God, and he shall be a governor in Judah, and Ekron as a Jebusite.

government and her subjugation ; the dwelling of an alien in Ashdod, is the banishment of the native population ; and the destruction of the pride of the Philistines, is the overthrow of those external means of attack and defence in which they placed their pride. History records the complete fulfilment of these prophecies. Of Gaza it is recorded that after a siege of two months it was taken, and the governor, or king Betis, dragged round the city ; a fact that may be, in part, referred to in the prediction, " a king shall perish from Gaza." In rendering מַמְזֵר " a bastard," our version has followed the Septuagint version of the word in Deut. 23 : 2, the only other text where it occurs. But the great majority of interpreters give it the meaning of alien, a foreigner.

V. 7. "And I will remove his blood from his mouth, and his abominations from between his teeth, and he that remains, even he, shall be for our God, and he shall be as a prince in Judah, and Ekron as the Jebusite."

The removal of his blood from his mouth, would seem, by the parallel phrase, to refer to the overthrow of idolatrous practices, one of which was the drinking of sacrificial blood.

In the clause, " and he that remains, even he, shall be for our God," it is intimated that this ruin shall not be total, but that some would remain, who should afterwards be converted to God. This conversion is illustrated by comparing those alluded to among the Philis-

8 And I will encamp about mine house because of the army, because of him that passeth by, and because of him that returneth : and no oppressor shall pass through them any more : for now have I seen with mine eyes.

tines to the Jebusites, who were incorporated into the Theocracy, after their subjugation by David. "Ekron as the Jebusite" is there explanatory of the same conversion that is expressed in the parallel clause, "he shall be a prince in Judah." This prediction received its fulfilment in the time of Christ, when a great multitude from Tyre and Sidon came to him, (Luke 6 : 17,) and when churches were planted along these coasts that Paul visited, and from which in the Dioclesian persecution there went up a great cloud of witnesses.

V. 8. "And I will encamp around my house because of the army, because of the passer by, and because of the returner, and the exactor shall no more pass through them, for now I see with mine eyes."

The question would naturally arise here to the Jew, will not this temple which we have built be in danger when such a conqueror is ravaging Palestine ? Is he not likely to attack Jerusalem, and undo all this work of our hands ? The prophet assures them that the temple is safe, because God will encamp around it, because of this invading army. And it is a remarkable fact, that when Alexander was advancing upon Jerusalem with great fury, he was arrested by a dream, and induced not only to spare it, but also to confer upon it great privileges. Hence in this narrowest sense the prediction has been completely verified.

K

But as the temple was only a symbol of the Church, the promise must have its widest fulfilment only in the glorious antitype, that Church that is kept as the apple of God's eye, and against which the gates of hell shall never prevail.

(1.) The condition of all men is laid open to the eye of God, and he will appoint judgment or mercy according to that condition, (v. 1.)

(2.) Worldly-wisdom is at last greatly inferior to that wisdom, the beginning of which is the fear of the Lord, (v. 2.)

(3.) However secure nations or men may think themselves in sin, their sin will be sure to find them out. Never has sin more proudly entrenched herself than in godless, but magnificent Tyre. Never has every element of earthly prosperity seemed more completely under control than in her case. And yet they were all swept like chaff before the whirlwind of the wrath of God, when the time for the fulfilment of his threatenings had come. Hence though nations now trample on law and right, and seem long to flourish in their sin, let not the child of God be impatient. Let him remember that two hundred years passed away after the utterance of these threatenings against Tyre, and she seemed stronger than ever, and yet when the day of doom had dawned, the galleys that left her on their stated voyages the peerless queen of the seas, when they returned found her but a bare and blackened rock, a lonely monument of the truth, that our God is a consuming fire. If, then, God thus executes his threats even on a mighty commonwealth, in spite of his delay, let not the fact that judgment against an evil work is not executed speedily cause the hearts of the sons of men to be fully set in them to do evil. Let men remember that it is a falsehood to violate a threatening as much as to violate a promise, and that God will not make himself a liar to save man in his sins, (v. 3—7.)

(4.) Amidst all the tumults of nations, the true people of God are safe, being guarded by the arm of Almightiness, (v. 8.)

II. The Lowly King Messiah.

Chapter 9 : 9, 10.

ANALYSIS.

I. A call to the Church to rejoice because of the coming of her King Messiah, (v. 9.)

II. The reasons for this rejoicing : (1.) His personal character (v. 9.) (2.) The nature and extent of his kingdom, (v. 10.)

That this passage applies to Christ is beyond all refutation. It was exactly fulfilled in his history, when he made his triumphal entry into Jerusalem, and is referred to him expressly by the Evangelist. (See Matt. 21 : 4, 5.) It contains expressions from older Messianic prophecies, the reference of which is generally admitted :

9 ¶ Rejoice greatly, O daughter of Zion ; shout, O daughter of Jerusalem ; behold, thy King cometh unto thee : he *is* just, and having salvation ; lowly, and riding upon an ass, and upon a colt the foal of an ass.

it was always so understood in the Jewish Church, until Christians used it as an argument in favor of Christ : and, finally, it can be consistently applied to none other. Hence, we are justified in taking it as a *jubilate*, addressed to the Church in view of her king, who is described as (1) just, (2) endowed with salvation, (3) lowly, (4) externally poor, "riding on an ass ;" and whose kingdom (v. 10) is declared as to its character to be peaceful, (v. 10,) and as to its extent, universal.

V. 9. "Rejoice greatly, daughter of Zion, shout for joy, daughter of Jerusalem, behold ! thy King cometh unto thee, just, and endowed with salvation, is he, lowly and riding upon an ass, and upon a foal, the son of she-asses."

The Theocracy, or Church, is called to rejoice because of the coming of her king. The kingly office of the Messiah, which was conferred upon him for the accomplishment of the work of redemption, is often alluded to as ground for rejoicing. (See Ps. 2, &c.) The ground of this rejoicing is expressed in the words succeeding, to be the character of the king, and the nature and extent of his kingdom.

(1.) He is "just." The righteousness here referred to is not his priestly, but his kingly righteousness, that rigorous justice of his reign in virtue of which no good should be unrewarded and no evil unpunished. In the unequal allotments of the present, when the good so often suffer and the bad so often escape. it is surely ground for rejoicing that the king, under whose rule this dispensation is placed, is just, and will render to every man according to his work.   This attribute is assigned to the Messiah also in Isa. 45 : 23 ; 53 : 11; Jer. 23 : 5 ; 33 : 15, &c.

(2.) He is "endowed with salvation." The word נוֹשָׁע is a difficult one here, and has received a great deal of attention from interpreters.   Being in the niphal or passive conjugation, it would literally be "saved," "protected," or "delivered." This would give a good sense, but rather a tame one, compared with the other characteristics named in the prophecy.   Hence it is usually taken in a secondary sense, as expressing not simply the reception of a salvation, but its possession as a gift that was capable of being bestowed upon others.   The same word occurs in this sense elsewhere, as Deut. 33 : 19 ; Ps. 33 : 16, &c.   The meaning then would be that God was with him, in spite of all his lowliness, sustaining him in the mighty work he had undertaken, and that this protection was bestowed upon him not as an individual but as a king, a representative of his people, so that he would not only enjoy it himself, but possess the power of bestowing it upon others.   Hence, while his inflexible justice might make us tremble in our sin, the fact that he was also endowed with a free salvation, and a salvation which he could bestow as a kingly right, would remove these fears and enable us to rejoice in this coming king.   This is the interpretation of this word by the LXX., the Targum, the Syriac, and Vulgate

versions, Bochart, Grotius, Marckius, Dathius, New-
come, Henderson, and Hengstenberg, with some slight
differences of opinion on a minor question of grammar.

(3.) He was to be "lowly." This word עָנִי is sometimes rendered meek, because of the Greek word used
in the quotation of this passage in Matt. 21 : 5, which
has this meaning. But as the word עָנִי always refers
to lowliness of outward circumstances, and עָנָו to lowliness of disposition, Hengstenberg and others allege
that the Evangelist did not mean to endorse the absolute accuracy of the Septuagint translation of the word,
but simply to quote it as a well-known version. If the
usual sense of the word be given, the Church would be
summoned to rejoice because of the humiliation of her
king. And however incongruous such a ground of rejoicing may seem to be to men generally, the heart
that is crushed with penitence or grief will comprehend
the reason of this summons. Had this august king
been as sorrowless as he was sinless, had he been a
robed seraph or a crowned monarch, the poor and suffering could never have approached him with confidence, for he could not have sympathized with them in
their sorrows. But when he comes to us as one who
can be touched with a feeling of our infirmities, we
welcome him with joy, and understand why we are
called to rejoice, because he comes to us as the lowly
king. It is marvellous that expositors should have
found so much difficulty here, when the reason of this
call to rejoice might have been found in the yearnings

10 And I will cut off the chariot from Ephraim, and the horse from Je-rusalem, and the battle bow shall be cut off : and he shall speak peace unto

of their own hearts for the sympathy of one who has himself tasted sorrow. Surely a suffering child of God can understand how blessed a thing it is to have a Saviour king who has known himself what it is to suffer.

(4.) He was to be externally in poverty, "riding upon an ass, and upon a foal, the son of she-asses." This is a prediction of poverty, for although in earlier times kings rode on asses, after the time of Solomon they were never so used, horses having taken their place. The employment of the horse in war also made the use of the ass an indication of peace as well as of poverty. The two members of the sentence are in the form of a climax, the use of an untrained colt being less honorable than that of a full-grown animal. The plural " she-asses," is merely the indefinite plural, as in Gen. 21 : 7, where "sons" is evidently used for the indefinite "son," since Sarah had but a single son. The exact fulfilment of this prophecy in the entrance of Christ into Jerusalem was merely a specific illustration of the general prediction, not the entire object of the prediction itself. Its range was much broader than this single event, and indeed would have been substantially fulfilled had this event never occurred. The specific fulfilment however rivets the prophecy more absolutely to Christ.

V. 10. " And I will cut off the chariot from Ephraim, and the horse from Jerusalem, and the bow of war shall be cut off, and he

the heathen ; and his dominion *shall*   river *even* to the ends of the earth.
be from sea *even* to sea, and from the

shall speak peace to the nations, and his dominion (*be*) from sea
to sea, and from the river to tħe ends of the earth."

V. 10 describes the peaceful character of the Messiah's kingdom in metaphorical terms, such as are used
elsewhere for the same purpose.   The chariot and horse
are of course those used in war, and their removal is
equivalent to the cessation of warfare.   The word
Ephraim here does not prove that this prophecy was
written before the exile, but only that the prophet was
familiar with the prophets of that period, and used
their language when he would describe the whole land
of Palestine.

The extent of this kingdom is indicated *first* by the
fact that he would " speak peace to the nations," (*Gentiles*,) and hence would rule beyond the limits of Israel ;
and *secondly*, by the phrase from " sea to sea," &c.,
which, by comparison with Ps. 72, and other passages,
will be found to express absolute universality, being
equivalent to the known world.   The Euphrates and
the Mediterranean were the geographical limits of the
earth as known to the Hebrews, and by introducing one
into the first member of the parallelism, and the other
into the second, the universality of the Messiah's kingdom was emphatically declared.

That the tendencies of Christ's kingdom are to universal peace and universal piety, we need not pause to
argue, and that these tendencies shall yet be fully em-

bodied, we believe as well from the voice of history as from the word of prophecy. We have only to patiently labor, and patiently wait, and the white banner of the lowly king shall in due time be unfurled from every mountain-top, and over every valley, and men be brother-murderers and brother-haters no more.

This beautiful prediction of the Messiah is a sort of episode, where the longings of prophecy for this mighty future seemed to burst forth, as if irrepressible. These involuntary gushings up of the prophetic hopes are exceedingly touching and beautiful. The prophet then returns to a nearer future in the succeeding verses.

PRACTICAL INFERENCES.

(1.) Christians should be happy. No people have a better right or better reason to rejoice, (v. 9.)

(2.) The righteousness wrought out by Christ is the great ground of his Kingly authority, (see Phil. 2 : 6—10,) and also of the joy of his people, (v. 9.)

(3.) A suffering people can find great comfort in the fact that they have a suffering Saviour ; see Heb. 4 : 15, (v. 9.)

(4.) Christians need never repine at earthly poverty when their King had not where to lay his head, (v. 9.)

(5.) War will cease on earth only when wickedness ceases, and wickedness will cease only when Christ's universal empire begins, (v. 10.)

11 As for thee also, by the blood of   prisoners out of the pit wherein *is* no
thy covenant I have sent forth thy   water.

III. THE MACCABEAN DELIVERANCE.

CHAPTER 9 : 11—17.

ANALYSIS.

I. The distress that would follow the Grecian conquests of
Alexander and his successors, (v. 11, 12.)

II. The wars occasioned by the revolt of the Jews under the
Maccabees, (v. 13—15.)

III. The Maccabean victories and their results, (v. 16, 17.)

THE key to this passage lies in v. 13, where a revolt
of the chosen people against the sons of Javan (Ionia or
Greece), is predicted.   There was no such collision between the Jews and the Greeks, except under the successors of Alexander.   Hence the prophecy must refer
to the times of the Maccabees.   It was natural that,
after predicting the conquests of Alexander, some allusion should be made to the important events succeeding.

V. 11. "Also thou—in the blood of thy covenant I have sent
forth thy prisoners, from the pit, and there is no water in it."

"Also thou"—   The prophet here turns to the
Theocracy to assure her that, in view of her covenant
relation, she should be delivered during the troublous
times that must precede the coming of the lowly king.
"In the blood of thy covenant," means on account of
the covenant sealed with blood, referring to the Sinaitic
covenant, which guaranteed protection to the chosen

12 ¶ Turn you to the strong hold,   I declare *that* I will render double unto
ye prisoners of hope : even to day do   thee ;

people while in the path of duty.   The imprisonment in
a pit where there was no water, is a metaphor drawn
from the deep wells often found in dungeons, into
which they lowered prisoners in special cases, and is a
figurative representation of the distress that would be
occasioned by the successors of Alexander.   How great
this distress was may be learned from history.   Palestine was the battle-ground of contending rivals for
empire, and suffered the usual calamities of such a position.   But these sufferings reached their height under
the ravages of the cruel Antiochus, who rifled and polluted the temple, murdered and enslaved thousands of
the people, and attempted to overturn the religion of
Jehovah, and establish the worship of Jupiter.   His
enormities were so great that the image of the prophet
was by no means exaggerated.   But these very severi-
ties were doubtless the means of preventing a national
apostasy.   The mild rule of the Ptolemies might soon
have seduced the Jews from their allegiance, but the
terrible persecutions of Antiochus only made them cling
more obstinately to the faith of their fathers.

V. 12. " Return to the strong hold, O prisoners of hope!   Even
to-day (*am I*) declaring, I will render double to you."

V. 12.   The image of the dungeon in v. 11, suggests
that of the strong hold, which is simply a metaphor for
divine deliverance.   God calls the people to return to
him, and he will protect them.   The phrase " prisoners

13 When I have bent Judah for me, filled the bow with Ephraim, and raised up thy sons, O Zion, against thy sons, O Greece, and made thee as the sword of a mighty man.

14 And the LORD shall be seen over them, and his arrow shall go forth as the lightning : and the Lord GOD shall blow the trumpet, and shall go with whirlwinds of the south.

of hope," means prisoners who have hope—a hope resting on the covenant. He then assures them that great as was their affliction, their prosperity should be doubly greater.

The next two verses are addressed to the Greeks, and declare, by two images, the deliverance that God would work. When it is remembered that at this time the Greeks were an obscure people, scarcely known beyond their own borders, this prophecy becomes one of the most remarkable in the Scriptures.

V. 13. "For I have bent to me Judah, the bow have I filled with Ephraim, and I have raised up thy sons, O Zion! against thy sons, O Javan! and have made thee as the sword of a mighty man."

V. 13. God appears here as a warrior, taking Judah for his bow, and Ephraim for his arrow, and bending the weapon against the enemies of Zion.

Then addressing Zion and Javan. alternately, he declares that he will make Zion like the sword of a mighty man, *i. e.* irresistible and invincible.

V. 14. "And over them Jehovah will appear, and his arrow goes forth like lightning, and the Lord Jehovah shall blow the trumpet, and he goes forth in the storms of the south."

V. 14 changes the image to that of a tempest, the arrowy flashes of whose lightning and the trumpet-peals of whose thunder, make it an army of resistless power.

15 The LORD of hosts shall defend them ; and they shall devour, and subdue with sling stones ; and they shall drink, *and* make a noise as through wine ; and they shall be filled like bowls, *and* as the corners of the altar.

16 And the LORD their God shall save them in that day as the flock of his people : for *they shall be as* the stones of a crown, lifted up as an ensign upon his land.

Storms of the south are violent storms, because such was their usual character, (see Isa. 21 : 1.)

V. 15. " Jehovah of Hosts will protect them, and they eat and they trample under foot the sling-stones, and they drink, and make a noise as from wine, and they are full as the altar-bowls, and as the corners of the altar."

V. 15 turns again to the covenant people, and describes them under the image of a lion, who devours his enemy and then treads him under foot. These enemies are represented under the image of sling-stones, to show their feebleness ; for only small stones were suitable for a sling ; stones which, when on the ground, were perfectly harmless. This lion was intoxicated with blood as with wine, filled with it like the bowls of the altar, and sprinkled with it, like the corners of the altar. These images of sanguinary conquest are very powerful.

V. 16. " And Jehovah their God will save them in that day, as a flock (*will he save*) his people, for as gems of a diadem are they lifted up in his land."

V. 16 contains yet other images of prosperity. God would not only give victory but afterwards peace, and hence the warrior and the lion are now exchanged for the shepherd and the flock, and the spent and worthless stones of the sling scornfully trampled under the feet,

17 For how great *is* his goodness,   shall make the young men cheerful,
and how great *is* his beauty! corn   and new wine the maids.

are contrasted with the brilliant and costly gems of the
diadem that are honorably placed upon the head.

V. 17. "For how great is his goodness ! and how great his
beauty ! Corn makes the young men to grow, and new wine the
maidens."

V. 17 is an exulting exclamation in view of the goodness and loveliness of God's character, and the blessings
he would then grant to the Theocracy. Corn and wine
indicated peace and prosperity that permitted the performance of agricultural labor, whilst the increase of
young men and maidens indicated the peaceful increase
of population, and showed that children were not cut
off, as they commonly are, in a state of war or trouble.

These images of prosperity predict the deliverance
that should take place under the Maccabees, which we
know to have been one of the most wonderful in history.
The tyranny of Antiochus aroused this brave family,
whose victories over the repeated armies sent to subdue
them, have no parallel but in the rapid conquests of
Alexander or Napoleon. Having retaken Jerusalem,
the temple was restored and the feast of the Purification
instituted, which connects itself with the history of our
Lord. The Maccabean rule was one of such prosperity
as to fulfil the terms of this prophecy, and designate its
era as one of the bright pages in the Hebrew annals.

The spiritual interpretations that are often given of
this passage, are not wholly accommodations of its

terms. All the facts of the Jewish history are looked at in their relation to the Messianic blessings, and have their value mainly in this connection, and hence as objects seen in the same plane and parallel, their outlines and lights are often blended. We, too, are often in a horrible pit and miry clay. We, too, are prisoners of hope, who are to go forth by the blood of the everlasting covenant ; and we, too, have an enemy more terrible by far than the gigantic Epiphanes, and are menaced with a storm of ruin more fearful than that which swept over widowed Judea. Hence the call to turn and flee to the strong hold, is one that may still be sounded to man, and the promised blessings of this passage shall but prefigure those greater blessings that shall be bestowed upon those who are the flock of the good shepherd, and who are among the jewels that glitter in his diadem of many crowns.

PRACTICAL INFERENCES.

(1.) The covenant love of God, and his faithful promises that are sealed with blood, are the hope of the Church in a time of trouble, (v. 11.)

(2.) Let sinners, who are also prisoners of hope, turn to the strong hold Christ, ere it be forever too late, and God will give them a double blessing, (v. 12.)

(3.) Men are only the instruments in God's hand for accomplishing his purposes, (v. 13.)

(4.) However terrific the tumult of wars and revolutions, the people of God are safe, (v. 14, 16.)

1 Ask ye of the LORD rain in the time of the latter rain ; *so* the LORD shall make bright clouds, and give them showers of rain, to every one grass in the field.

(5.) After the storm comes the rainbow. After the tears of suffering faith, comes the radiance of joyful hope, (v. 17.)

IV. PRAYER AND PROMISE.

CHAPTER 10 : 1—5.

ANALYSIS.

I. The call to prayer, because (1) thus God would bestow blessing, (v. 1); (2) their former objects of worship were false, (v. 2); (3) their former rulers were wicked, (v. 3.)

II. Promise of blessings in answer to prayer ; (1) rulers from themselves (v. 4); (2) conquest of their enemies, (v. 5.)

V. 1. " Ask of Jehovah rain, in the time of the latter rain ; Jehovah shall (*then*) cause lightnings, and shall give abundant rain, to every man grass in his field."

WE have here expressed the connection between prayer and promise on the one hand, and prayer and the processes of nature on the other. The blessing of rain, which to an agricultural people, was inclusive of all other temporal blessings, and symbolical of all spiritual ones, was promised ; but this promise was dependent on its supplication in prayer. Just as in the great blessing of the descent of the spirit on an individual or a Church, though a free gift, it must be obtained by prayer. It is this fact that makes the spirit of prayer

2 For the idols have spoken vanity, and the diviners have seen a lie, and have told false dreams ; they comfort in vain : therefore they went their way as a flock, they were troubled, because *there was* no shepherd.

in the Church an index at once of her piety, and of the spiritual blessings she may expect from God. When the Church pours out a fulness of prayer, God will pour out a fulness of his spirit. The inspired writers see no difficulty in the connection between prayer and the processes of nature, such as the mole-eyed philosophy of modern times discovers. They think that the God who has created the elements, may direct them according to his will. "The latter rain" was that which fell in March, to ripen the harvest, whose seed had been watered by the former rain in October. We must not suppose that because God has begun to bless us, we may relax our prayers and efforts. The former rain may be given, but we must also ask for the latter rain. We may have the former rain of conversion, but if we would have the latter rain of ripened sanctification of nature, we must continue to ask of God. So, also, in the revival of religion. The former rain may occur, and souls be converted, but if we would have the ripening of the seed in active Christians, we must ask of God, and he will give growth, greenness and maturity.

V. 2. " For the teraphim speak nothingness ; and the soothsayers see falsehood ; and the dreams speak vanity ; they comfort falsely ; wherefore they wander as a flock, they are troubled because there is no shepherd."

V. 2 gives the reason for that suffering of the Jews that made God's interposition necessary. They had

L

3 Mine anger was kindled against the shepherds, and I punished the goats ; for the LORD of hosts hath visited his flock the house of Judah, and hath made them as his goodly horse in the battle.

4 Out of him came forth the corner, out of him the nail, out of him the

forsaken God for other sources of light, and hence soon found themselves in darkness and emptiness. It is a mournful proof of man's depravity that he will believe any one sooner than God, and seek comfort anywhere rather than from heaven. But when men resort to their earthly teraphim, they find at last that they have been deceived, and are left in loneliness and sorrow. So it was with the Jews. They wandered like silly sheep, and soon found themselves among the wild mountains and the howling beasts of prey. The teraphim were the household gods of the heathen, some sort of images, the form and character of which we do not know. The etymology of the word is uncertain.

V. 3. " Against the shepherds my anger is kindled, and the he-goats will I punish, for Jehovah of Hosts visits his flock, the house of Judah, and makes them like a caparisoned horse in war."

The people had shepherds, but they were false ones, and they are here threatened. " The he-goats " are the leaders of the people, an image taken from the flock which the he-goats usually head, as they move from place to place. They who are first in crime, will be first in punishment. But God will visit his flock in mercy, and make each one, instead of a timid sheep, to be a war-horse, decked for the battle.

V. 4. " From him (is) the corner-stone, and from him the pin, from him the bow of battle, from him comes forth every ruler together."

battle bow, out of him every oppressor together.

5 ¶ And they shall be as mighty *men*, which tread down *their enemies* in the mire of the streets in the battle : and they shall fight, because the LORD *is* with them, and the riders on horses shall be confounded.

V. 4 predicts that the rulers of the country shall then come forth from the people themselves, and not from foreigners. These are called corner-stones and pins, which were used to suspend things upon, because such men were the support of the State, on which everything was sustained or suspended. So, from themselves should come forth military deliverers, symbolized by the "battle-bow." All this was literally fulfilled in the times of the Maccabees, but receives its highest fulfilment in the self-sustaining energy and resources of the kingdom of Messiah.

V. 5. "And they shall be as heroes, trampling on the mire of the streets in war, and they fight, for Jehovah is with them, and the riders on horses are put to shame."

V. 5 predicts the conquests of the chosen people, that they will trample down their enemies as mire in the streets, and overcome cavalry, so formidable usually to the infantry of the Jews. The cavalry of Antiochus was thus trampled down by the resistless ranks of the the Maccabean armies. But, as in previous cases, for reasons already given, these temporal blessings of the Theocracy but symbolize the higher blessings of the Church, whose triumphs are bloodless and tearless, and whose strength is that of the spirit, mighty to the pulling down of strong holds, and the subduing of principalities and powers.

PRACTICAL INFERENCES.

(1.) Prayer and promise are the two wires of the telegraph between earth and heaven, the one coming forth from the lips of man, the other from the lips of God, (v. 1.)

(2.) Prayer for promised blessings is as needful as the promise itself, for it is the condition of its performance ; the time of the latter rain may have come, and yet we must ask for it, (v. 1.)

(3.) All the laws of nature are as completely under the control of God now as when they were originally impressed, and can be turned to the answer of prayer as readily as to the reward of right doing in any other form, (v. 1.)

(4.) All comfort in religion is not true comfort, for it may rest on an error or a heresy, that shall be proved false at last, (v. 2.)

(5.) Rulers who are first in doing, will also be first in suffering, if this doing is wrong-doing, (v. 3.)

(6.) God is in human history, (v. 4, 5.)

V. The Restoration of the Jews.

Chapter 10 : 6—12.

ANALYSIS.

I. The permanent establishment of the two great divisions of the chosen people in their own land, (v. 6, 7.)

II. The causes of this restoration, (1) God's redeeming work (v. 8;) (2) their penitence, (v. 9.)

III. The extent of this restoration reaching to all possible places of dispersion, (v. 10, 11.)

IV. The conversion of the Jews, (v. 12.)

————

THE prophets do not observe an exact chronological order in their prophecies, but often group together the nearer and more remote. Like a painter who in depicting a landscape will put on the same canvas the hillock at his feet and the mountain that lies leagues away, so they often place the remotest objects in immediate proximity to the nearest in sketching their wondrous pictures. This arises partly, from the nature of the prophetic vision that saw future events as it were in the same plane ; partly, from the fact that the greater future was connected with the lesser present by some bond of relation, causal or otherwise, and hence ought to be considered in connection with it ; and partly, from the fact that we naturally rise to the great future, even though but imperfectly connected with the present, when we would draw encouragement to bear existing toils and trials. Thus it is with the minister of the gospel now, who continually breaks away from the narrow present to the more glorious future, either on earth or in heaven, and thus naturally would it be with the prophets of the Old Testament. Hence we need not be surprised to find a mingling of events in the same prophecy that are very remote in their chronological relations. Such is the case in the present instance, where the restoration of the Jews, an event

6 And I will strengthen the house of Judah, and I will save the house of Joseph, and I will bring them again to place them; for I have mercy upon them: and they shall be as though I had not cast them off; for I *am* the LORD their God, and will hear them.

7 And *they of* Ephraim shall be like a mighty *man*, and their heart shall rejoice as through wine: yea, their children shall see *it*, and be glad; their heart shall rejoice in the LORD.

still future, is connected with the Maccabean deliverance, an event long since past. Like the near planet and the remote fixed star, though widely different and widely apart, they are seen as if side by side in the prophetic firmament.

Henderson follows Grotius in supposing that this restoration took place before the coming of Christ, but the terms in which it is described can hardly be restricted to any return that took place during that period. Calvin refers it entire to a spiritual restoration. But the most natural interpretation seems to be that which predicts a future return to their own land, and a spiritual return to God, which is predicted as a separate and ultimate result in v. 12.

V. 6. " And I will strengthen the house of Judah, and I will save the house of Joseph, and I will again cause them to dwell, for I have compassion upon them ; and they shall be as though I had not cast them out, for I am Jehovah their God, and I will hear them."

V. 6 declares the permanent establishment of the two tribes, and the reason of it found in their covenant relation to God, and his compassion on them.

V. 7. "And Ephraim shall be as a mighty man, their heart shall rejoice as (*with*) wine, and their sons shall see and rejoice, their heart shall rejoice in Jehovah."

8 I will hiss for them, and gather them; for I have redeemed them: and they shall increase as they have increased.

9 And I will sow them among the people: and they shall remember me in far countries; and they shall live with their children, and turn again.

V. 7 extends the same blessing to Ephraim, the most prominent of the ten tribes, most of whom had not yet returned from captivity, and hence needed encouragement.

V. 8. "I will hiss to them and collect them, for I have redeemed them, and they shall be many as they were before."

V. 8 begins to widen the view to include the great restoration. "I will hiss to them," is an image taken from the management of bees, where the apiarist hisses or whistles to collect the swarm. It is designed to express the ease with which a work, seemingly so difficult, could be accomplished. God has only to hiss and these scattered exiles will be brought back. The word "redeemed" and the context show that this restoration is connected with their conversion to God.

V. 9. "And I will sow them among the peoples, and in distant lands they shall remember me, and with their children they shall live and return."

V. 9 shows that the dispersion alluded to was with a special design. They were "sown," and like seed long buried in the dust, they are awaiting the time of germination. It may also indicate the future use of the Jews, when this germ of vitality shall be awakened, in extending the knowledge of the true God as missionaries. The slight hold that they have on every soil where they now live, the commercial, and hence cosmo-

10 I will bring them again also out of the land of Egypt, and gather them out of Assyria ; and I will bring them into the land of Gilead and Lebanon ; and *place* shall not be found for them.

11 And he shall pass through the sea with affliction, and shall smite the waves in the sea, and all the deeps of the river shall dry up ; and the pride of Assyria shall be brought down, and the sceptre of Egypt shall depart away.

politan character of their pursuits, making a change of residence so easy to them, fit them peculiarly for missionary work. If converted generally, they would be a seed of great power in almost every nation of the world. The mention of their children indicates the completeness and permanence of this restoration.

V. 10. " And I will bring them back from the land of Egypt, and from Assyria will I gather them, and to the land of Gilead and Lebanon will I bring them, and there shall not be room to contain them."

V. 10 proves that this dispersion alluded to here is not the Babylonish captivity, but a later and wider one. Egypt and Assyria are taken as types of all the lands of their dispersion, the one being the first great oppressor of the chosen people and the other among the last, and the one lying on the north whilst the other lay on the south. Hence they are here taken merely as types of the universal dispersion, just as Shinar in ch. 5 : 11. So in the next clause, Gilead beyond Jordan, and Lebanon on the hither side, represent the entire land of promise.

V. 11. "And he passes through the sea, the affliction, and he smites in the sea the waves, and all the deeps of the river are put to shame, and the pride of Assyria is overthrown, and the rod of Egypt shall give way."

V. 11, keeping up the allusions of v. 10, employs the

12 And I will strengthen them   up and down in his name, saith the
in the LORD; and they shall walk   LORD.

passage of the Red Sea as an image of the future de-
liverances of the great restoration. "He" probably
refers to God, and "affliction" is in apposition with
"sea," showing that it is to be taken metaphorically and
not literally. Smiting the waves in the sea, is stilling
them, putting down all opposition. "The river" is
either the Nile or the Tigris; if the latter, its peculiar
importance as a means of defence to Nineveh may be
alluded to. "The rod of Egypt shall give way" is of
course a metaphorical statement of the fact that the
power of all enemies to restrain and oppress the chosen
people would be forced to relax. The general meaning of the verse is that all future obstacles would be as
powerless to arrest this return as the Red Sea and Jordan were to prevent that of their fathers.

V. 12. "And I will strengthen them in Jehovah, and in his
name shall they walk, saith Jehovah."

V. 12 predicts their conversion. Here again we find
one Jehovah speaking of another, and predicting the
fact that in the name they now despise and hate, they
shall walk, and shall bear that name with joy. They
shall call themselves Christians, for as it is in Christ
that they are to be strengthened, he is this Jehovah.

PRACTICAL INFERENCES.

(1.) Christians should pray for the conversion of the
Jews, since that conversion is promised. We must pray

for rain in the time of the latter rain. It was stated in 1853, that the latter rain had appeared in Palestine the previous year, for the first time since the downfall of Jerusalem. If this be true, it would indicate a reason for prayer that the latter rain of the Spirit may be poured out, according to promise, (v. 1.)

(2.) The dispersion of the Jews during nearly two thousand years, for the crime of rejecting Christ, proves that this crime is one of no ordinary magnitude, and that it is a fearful thing to bear the rejected blood of the Redeemer. If these things were done in a green tree, what shall be done in a dry? (v. 8, 9.)

(3.) When the fulness of time comes, all the difficulties in the way of fulfilling God's promises shall melt away, (v. 10, 11.)

(4.) There are evidently two Jehovahs spoken of in v. 12, one of whom is the speaker, and the other spoken of. Hence there are either two Gods, which leads us to polytheism, or two persons of the same Godhead, which leads us to the doctrine of the New Testament, that Christ, in whom all the redeemed are at last to be saved, is Jehovah, God over all, blessed forever, (v. 12.)

VI. The Mission of Messiah.

Chapter 11.

ANALYSIS.

I. The troubles that would precede the coming of Christ under the image of a storm, (11 : 1—3.)

II. The coming of Christ to make one last effort to save the covenant people. (1) The call to the shepherd to take charge of the flock, (v. 4—6.) (2) His answer to that call, and actual assumption of the pastoral office, (v. 7, 8.) (3) His rejection and sale for thirty pieces of silver, (v. 9—14.)

III. The curse that would follow this rejection, under the symbol of an evil shepherd who oppresses the flock and is afterwards punished, (v. 14—17.)

In the utterances of God to his people, the voice of Ebal is always set over against that of Gerizim, and the blessing to faithfulness is enforced by the curse against unfaithfulness. This is necessary, owing to our proneness to sever the blessing from that obedience which is its condition, and expect the one whilst we neglect the other. It is therefore necessary for God to show us that in the same cloud where the rain is treasured there also sleeps the thunderbolt. Hence after promising (chap. 10 : 1,) the refreshing showers, on the condition of fidelity, the prophet now turns to the stormy rush of evils that would come in their place, if they were unfaithful. These evils are described in a highly dramatic form in ch. 11.

1 Open thy doors, O Lebanon, that the fire may devour thy cedars.

2 Howl, fir tree ; for the cedar is fallen ; because the mighty are spoil-

Part 1. *The storm preceding the coming of Christ,* v. 1—3.

V. 1—3. " Open, O Lebanon, thy gates, and let the fire consume thy cedars. Howl, O cypress, for the cedar falls, for the lofty are laid waste ; howl, O ye oaks of Bashan, for the thick forest falls. A voice of howling of the shepherds, for their glory is laid waste : a voice of roaring of the lions, for the pride of Jordan is laid waste."

Henderson follows most of the interpreters in referring this passage to the temple. The Jews, generally, so explained it, and nearly all the Christian expositors have followed them. But Calvin properly remarks that it is a most frigid interpretation, and hence gives the true view, which has been followed by Hengstenberg, and a few others, that it is a prediction of tumult and trouble, under the image of a storm traversing the whole land of Palestine.

It is a highly dramatic passage. The prophet looks to the north, and sees sweeping down a terrific tempest, that bursts through the rocky ramparts of Lebanon, consumes with its lightnings the lordly cedars, lays waste the lofty monarchs of the forest, and spreads terror and ruin along its track. The cypress is called to tremble, because the mightier cedar has been unable to withstand the shock, and the oaks of Bashan to fear because the dense and firmly knit forest has been prostrated by its rush. There mingles then with the crash of the storm a voice of terror and despair from the shepherds who see their broad pastures laid waste ; and a cry of rage and fear from the lions as their lairs on

ed ; howl, O ye oaks of Bashan, for the forest of the vintage is come down.

3 ¶ *There is* a voice of the howling of the shepherds ; for their glory is spoiled ; a voice of the roaring of young lions ; for the pride of Jordan is spoiled.

the banks of the Jordan are torn up by the sweep of the hurricane. " The pride of Jordan," is a well-known phrase for the beautiful shrubbery that lined its bank, in whose tangled recesses the wild beast found a shelter. The passage is a bold and beautiful description of a tempest that sweeps over the entire length and breadth of the holy land, prostrating everything before it. This metaphor describes the storm of invasion, bloodshed and oppression that should roll over Palestine after the glorious Maccabean era, and before the coming of the Messiah. The designation of Lebanon and Bashan belong to the metaphor, and not to the fulfilment, being designed to set forth by the usual course of such storms the track of this tempest, and hence it is not necessary for us to show that any invasions actually came by the way of Lebanon. The reference is to that desolating storm of civil war that caused the calling in of the Romans, whose legions swept like a whirlwind of steel over the land, and finally prostrated every vestige of independent authority, from the cedar of Lebanon to the lowliest cypress, from the peaceful shepherd to the lion-like spirit that refused to be subdued, and humbled the whole land beneath the mighty power of Rome. It was this state of deep prostration that constituted the dark hour before the dawn, the fulness of time on the arrival of which the great shepherd was to come. God

4 Thus saith the LORD my God ; Feed the flock of the slaughter ;
5 Whose possessors slay them, and hold themselves not guilty ; and they that sell them say, Blessed *be* the LORD; for I am rich, and their own shepherds pity them not.

had sent messenger after messenger, some of kindness, and some of wrath, but at that time he would make one more effort, and send forth his own son, made of a woman, made under the law, saying, "surely they will reverence my son."

Part 2.   Christ assumes the pastoral care of the Theocracy.

V. 4—14.

The prophet here appears as a type of Christ, and performs a series of symbolic actions that represent the advent of the Messiah "to his own," and his rejection by them, with its bitter consequences.   One last effort will be made to rescue them from the wrath they are so recklessly braving.   By remembering that this whole passage is a dramatic representation, in which the prophet acts as a type of Christ, in the first instance, and of the foolish shepherd in the second, the interpretation will be clear and easy.

V. 4. " Thus saith Jehovah my God, Feed the flock of slaughter."

V. 4.   " Flock of slaughter " is a flock doomed or sentenced to slaughter, in consequence of their insane rejection of the care of the good shepherd.   During the war with the Romans, and the capture of Jerusalem by Titus, a million and a half of the Jews were slaughtered.

V. 5. " Whose buyers slaughter them, and do not become guilty ; and whose sellers say, blessed be Jehovah, for I am enriched, and their shepherds spare them not."

6 For I will no more pity the inhabitants of the land, saith the LORD; but lo, I will deliver the men every one into his neighbor's hand, and into the hand of his king; and they shall smite the land, and out of their hand I will not deliver *them*.

V. 5 expresses the thought that, although once they who oppressed the covenant people would be guilty and so treated by God, now the sins of the people were such that these oppressions were righteous punishments, and their agents therefore not guilty for the execution itself, however they might be for the mode and motives with which they performed it. By the buyers and sellers are meant the Romans, who used the Jews, as they did all their conquests, as mere merchandise, making from them the greatest possible gain for themselves. "Their shepherds" refer to the civil and ecclesiastical rulers of the Jews, and there is predicted here that extortion and treachery in which the Pharisee and Sadducee wrung from the unhappy people what the Roman had failed to extort, and both combined thus in spite of their mutual hate in this work of shameless robbery.

V. 6. "For I will no longer spare the dwellers in this land, saith Jehovah, And behold! I will give up each man to the hand of his neighbor, and to the hand of his king, and they lay waste the land, and I will not deliver out of their hand."

V. 6 gives the reason for making this last effort to save them; their wickedness could no longer be borne, but must be arrested either by penitence at the call of Christ, or punishment at the sword of the Roman. The nature of the punishment is described in the latter clauses. Civil war and intestine discord are delineated

7 And I will feed the flock of slaugh-ter, *even* you, O poor of the flock. And I took unto me two staves ; the one I called Beauty, and the other I called Bands ; and I fed the flock.

in each man being given into " the hand of his neighbor," whilst the Roman oppression is indicated by " the hand of the king." Both these were fulfilled in those fearful times when the bloody factions that wasted the land found but a single bond of union, and that in their common hate of their rightful king, and their prophetic cry, " we have no king but Cæsar."

V. 7. " So I fed the flock of slaughter, in order that (*I might preserve*) the humble of the flock. And I took to myself two staves, the one I called Favor, the other I called Union, and I fed the flock."

V. 7 represents Christ as taking by covenant the mediatorial work, and gives his reason for so doing. That reason is contained in the phrase, " therefore the humble of the flock." This phrase presents no little grammatical difficulty. The word לָכֵן is taken by our translators and others as a pronoun with the preposition לְ prefixed, and rendered as a dative of advantage, "for you," *i. e.*, for your sakes, " I will feed the flock." This is the sense of the passage, but it requires us to assume a form of the pronoun that never occurs elsewhere. Henderson, and others, take it as a participial noun, in the sense of " truly," לְ being considered as redundant. This gives a good sense, but a more unusual meaning to the word, and does not cohere with the context so well, unless we render עֲנִי " miserable," which is not its proper meaning here, (see v. 11.) Others translate it as an adverb, rendering it "because." This would give the exact sense, but this word, in strictness, never has the sense of "because," but always that of "therefore." But there are cases in which it is used to introduce not only the cause but the design of an action. (See Alexander on Isa. 26 : 14.) Taking it in this sense it would furnish the design with which Christ fed the flock, namely, to feed or save "the humble of the flock," the remnant of faithful ones who had never bowed the knee to Baal. We have rendered עֲנִיֵּי by "humble," because it has that double sense of outward lowliness and inward meekness that עֲנִי has, especially in this passage. This portion of the flock is referred to in v. 11 more explicitly as the humble of the flock who clung to the Messiah. Hence the fact is set forth, that Christ assumed the work of feeding the Jewish people, in order that he might save that remnant of them who were waiting for the salvation of Israel. Had there not been such a remnant, he would have come as an avenging instead of a suffering messenger from God.

The assumption of this work is symbolically represented by taking two staves of office, or crooks, such as shepherds usually carried. One was called *Favor*, (Eng. version, *Beauty*,) and symbolised the favor with which God caused the Jews to be regarded by other nations, and their rights respected until the work of redemption was completed. How marvellously they were thus preserved, with all their records, usages, and institutions, until "the son of David" came, is well known. Alex-

M

8 Three shepherds also I cut off in   and their soul also abhorred me.
one month; and my soul loathed them,   9 Then said I, I will not feed you:

ander, Antiochus and Pompey, were alike held back from destroying them until the mystic staff was broken, after which the power of Titus and the malignity of Julian were alike impotent even to save or restore their temple. The second staff was called *Union*, (Eng. version, *Bands*,) and symbolised that union within themselves, which was secured until the coming of Christ, in order that it could be seen that all the words of prophecy in regard to him were minutely fulfilled.

V. 8. "And I destroyed three shepherds in one month, and my soul was grieved with them, and their soul abhorred me."

V. 8. "I destroyed three shepherds in one month." The obscurity of this phrase would have been more easily removed by interpreters, if the three-fold nature of Christ's work had been recollected, and its relation to the Jewish polity. He was the great antetype, of which that polity was the complex type. Now he, as our Redeemer, appeared as a Prophet, a Priest and a King, and thus fulfilled all the significance of these three orders in the old dispensation. He was the promised prophet, the one and only priest, and the king in Zion, and hence his appearing brought these respective orders in the theocracy to an end, since they were only designed to foreshadow his advent and kingdom. This was done in judicial anger also; they were deposed because of their unfaithfulness in the discharge of their duties. "One month" is mentioned to show that this was done

that that dieth, let it die ; and that   and let the rest eat, every one the flesh
that is to be cut off, let it be cut off;   of another.

gradually and yet not protractedly. A month is the
intermediate measure of time between a day and a year,
and expresses thus that gradual transition from the old
to the new dispensation, which did in fact occur. The
one overlapped and evolved the other

The other clauses of the verse represent that mutual
aversion that existed between Christ and the magnates
of the Jewish people. He denounced them with terrible severity, as vipers, hypocrites, &c., whilst they hated
him so that they even gloated in fiendish delight over
his agony on the cross.

V. 9. "Then I said, I will not feed you, the dying, let them die,
the cut off, let them be cut off, the remaining, let them consume
each the flesh of the other."

V. 9 sets forth the final abandonment of the Jewish
people to their fate, when it became evident that they
would not listen to the voice of Jesus. They were left
to their fatal choice. A threefold calamity is predicted ;
pestilence and famine, "the dying ;" war, "the cut off ;"
and intestine discord, "let them consume each the flesh
of the other." How terribly these predictions were fulfilled may be seen from the pages of Josephus, where
this threefold calamity is set forth in the most appalling
details, in relating the history of the latter days of the
Jewish republic.

V 10. " And I took my staff Favor and brake it ; to abolish my
covenant that I had made with all nations."

10 ¶ And I took my staff, *even* Beauty, and cut it asunder, that I might break my covenant which I had made with all the people.

11 And it was broken in that day: and so the poor of the flock that waited upon me knew that it *was* the word of the LORD.

V. 10 refers to that period when God let loose the angry nations of the earth against his people, and removed that girdle of protection that he had so long kept around them. This is symbolised by breaking the staff *Favor*, which is explained as abolishing the covenant that God had made with all nations. This covenant was of course not a formal engagement between God and all nations in favor of the Jews, but an ordinance of God in reference to all nations, by which they were restrained from destroying the Jews. A similar form of speech will be found in Hos. 2 : 20, when God makes a covenant with the beasts, the birds, and the insects, and in Job 5 : 23, which speaks of a covenant with the stones of the field. This was fulfilled when the Roman eagles gathered in hungry ferocity about the dying commonwealth.

V. 11. "And it (*the covenant*) was abolished in that day, and thus they knew, (*viz.*) the humble of the flock who clung to me, that this is the word of Jehovah."

V. 11 states that when this protection was withdrawn "the humble of the flock" who clung to Christ should know that this was the word of Jehovah. This was remarkably fulfilled. When Jerusalem was compassed with armies, the Christians remembered the warning of Christ to flee to the mountains, and accordingly when Titus unaccountably raised the siege for a few days, as

12 And I said unto them, If ye think good, give *me* my price; and if not, forbear. So they weighed for my price thirty *pieces* of silver.

if to give them an opportunity of obeying Christ's words, they fled to Pella, and escaped the fate of those who remained in the city. Thus they knew that this was the word of Jehovah.

V. 12. "Then I said to them, if it seem good in your eyes, give me my reward, and if not, withhold it, and they weighed my reward, thirty pieces of silver !"

V. 12 contains the record of the final rejection of Christ. The expression, "if it seem good in your eyes," &c., is one of indignant contempt, with an intimation that to retain that reward was a far more costly thing than to bestow it. The reward was that travail of his soul which it was promised he should see and be satisfied, when men would receive him as a Saviour from sin. They, however, not only withheld that obedience and love that were the proper return for the work of Christ among them, but they added insult to injury. "They weighed," (alluding to the ancient mode of computing the value of money,) "my reward, thirty pieces of silver." This was the price of a servant who was gored by an ox, (see Ex. 21 : 32,) a fact that made the sum a gross insult to him who was the Lord of all. How exactly this was fulfilled, when the traitor sold his master for thirty pieces of silver, all now know. It was fulfilled in its very minutest particulars.

V. 13. "And Jehovah said to me, Cast it to the potter, this magnificent price at which I was valued of them, and I took the thirty

13 And the Lord said unto me, Cast the thirty *pieces* of silver, and cast them
it unto the potter : a goodly price that to the potter in the house of the Lord.
I was prized at of them.   And I took

pieces of silver, and I cast it down in the house of Jehovah, *(to
be given thence)* to the potter."

V. 13 shows what was to be done with this price,
which is ironically called a "magnificent price." It was
to be cast to the potter.   This was a proverbial phrase
for cast it to an unclean place, like our phrases, "throw
it to the dogs," "to the moles and the bats," and others
of like character.   The origin of this proverb was in the
fact that the potter for the temple had his shop in the
valley of Hinnom, because it furnished the most suitable
clay for his purpose.   This valley was a polluted place
to the Jews, because of the idolatry once practiced
there, and also because of the fact that Josiah defiled it
with carrion, bones, &c.   See 2 Kings 23 : 10.   Hence
to cast a thing to the potter, was to cast it to the valley
of Hinnom, or to intimate that it was an unclean and
unholy thing.   That it was to be cast there, was because
of a prophecy in Jer., chs. 18th and 19th, where the
valley of Hinnom and the shop of the potter are
taken as scenes for symbolic actions that apply to this
precise period of Jewish history.   The prophet Zechariah mentions the potter to connect this prophecy with
the older one of Jeremiah, and show that it was only a
fuller development of it, or more strictly a second and
wider execution of the threatening then contained
against unfaithfulness.   That this view of the relation
of the later to the earlier prophecy is correct, is proved

by Matt. 27 : 9, where it is said, " Then was fulfilled that which was spoken by Jeremy the prophet, saying, And they took the thirty pieces of silver, the price of him that was valued, whom they of the children of Israel did value, and gave them for the potter's field as the Lord appointed me." The very fact that seems at first sight a difficulty, is the one that proves this connection. It will be seen that the words of Zechariah are referred to Jeremiah, and this is the uniform reading of all the best MSS. of the gospel. Why then is the prophecy referred to Jeremiah? For the very same reason that a man quoting from the abridgement of a law book, would probably refer to the original author rather than the compiler, even though he quoted the words of the compilation. This is not a solitary instance in the New Testament writers. Mark 1 : 2, 3, quotes the words of Malachi, and refers them to Isaiah, to show the relation between the prophecies. So it is here. The passage is quoted, not verbatim, but with slight explanatory variations, as if to suggest to the reader the fact meant to be indicated by connecting the name of the earlier prophet with the form of the prediction that was given in the words of the later. This was much more obvious to the Jews than it is to us, because the minor prophets were all regarded as constituting but one book, and hence rarely quoted by name, and regarded as supplemental and subsidiary to the major prophets. Hence we see how wonderfully the prediction and the fulfil-

14 Then I cut asunder mine other | the brotherhood between Judah and
staff, *even* Bands, that I might break | Israel.

ment have been connected in their very minutest terms, and their very obscurest intimations.

It ought to be remarked, however, that the majority of commentators prefer the supposition that there has been a mistake of the transcribers, and that Jeremiah has been written for Zechariah in the contracted form, or that a marginal reference to Jeremiah has crept into the text, the Evangelist having originally written only "the prophet" without giving any name, the view held by Augustine. Either of these suppositions is probable, and if supported by external evidence, would be admissible. But in view of the changes made by Matthew in quoting the text, and the connection actually existing between the two passages as predictions of the same period, the opinion of Hengstenberg, which is given above, seems to be the most probable.

V. 14. "And I broke my second staff Union, to destroy the brotherhood between Judah and Israel."

V. 14 predicts by the symbol of breaking the second staff Union, the intestine discord that raged so fearfully after the rejection of Christ by the Jews. The destruction of the brotherhood between Judah and Israel is not to be taken literally, for this bond had been broken long before in the time of Rehoboam, but is used as a metaphor of disunion. The breach of the past, with its mournful results, is used as a type of the future. How terribly this prediction was fulfilled can be seen in the

15 ¶ And the LORD said unto me, Take unto thee yet the instruments of a foolish shepherd.

16 For lo, I will raise up a shepherd in the land, *which* shall not visit those that be cut off, neither shall seek the

pages of Josephus. The most terrible factions that have ever torn out the vitals of a commonwealth appeared in Judea, and amidst the terrors of invasion without and the horrors of fratricide within, this prophecy was fulfilled. The staff of protection from evil abroad and the staff of continued union at home were both broken, and the double horrors of foreign and domestic war paid the fearful penalty of rejecting the Lord of life, and setting upon him a price which in itself was an insult, and a mockery.

Part 3. The curse of evil rulers after the rejection of Christ.

CH. 11 : 15—*end.*

These verses describe a second symbolic action, in which the prophet predicts the curse of evil rulers by taking the implements of a foolish shepherd. What these were we are not told, but they were doubtless implements calculated to injure and destroy, rather than to benefit the flock. He thus declared that after rejecting their rightful Lord, God would send upon them wicked and cruel rulers, who would waste and scatter them.

V. 15. " And Jehovah said to me, again, take to thee the implements of a foolish shepherd."

V. 15. "Again," seems to be spoken to the prophet and to summon him to the resumption of those sym-

young one, nor heal that that is broken, nor feed that that standeth still : but he shall eat the flesh of the fat, and tear their claws in pieces.

bolical actions that were connected with the predictions, and that now were to express a new state of facts.

V. 16. "For behold! I raise up a shepherd in the land. The perishing will he not visit, the straying will he not seek out, the wounded will he not heal, the feeble will he not nourish, and the flesh of the fat ones will he eat, and their hoofs will he break off."

V. 16. "The shepherd in the land," is of course not to be taken as an individual, but as representing the ruling power, in whomsoever vested. The character- istics of that power would be neglect, greediness and cruelty. The perishing, straying, wounded and feeble, who needed his aid, would be neglected, whilst the fat ones would be devoured, and adding cruelty to greed, their very hoofs would be broken off.

Henderson restricts this verse to Herod, but without sufficient reason. Herod was undoubtedly included, but to limit it to him would restrict the threatening to the time of the advent, instead of extending it, where it undoubtedly reaches, to the downfall of the Hebrew commonwealth.

V. 17. "Wo to the worthless shepherd, forsaking the flock ! A sword upon his arm ! and upon his right eye ! His arm shall surely be withered, and his right eye shall surely be blind."

V. 17 declares that these rulers themselves should not escape, but the arm that oppressed should be pal- sied, and the eye that coveted should be blinded.

The reference here seems mainly, though not exclu- sively to be to the Romans. They were the rulers, but

17 Wo to the idol shepherd that leaveth the flock! the sword *shall be* upon his arm, and upon his right eye: his arm shall be clean dried up, and his right eye shall be utterly darkened.

not the only rulers of the Jewish people. They were at once rapacious, proud and cruel, and they thronged like vultures to batten on the yet quivering flesh of the dying commonwealth. But they in turn were assailed by others, and it is by overlooking the very exactness of the fulfilment of the terms of the prophecy that the query has been raised about their significance. It is said that there is an incongruity in the change of punishment predicted, the first words declaring that it shall be the sword, and the next that it shall be palsy and blindness. But this will vanish the moment we look at the exact facts of the case. Rome, like some old lion who had ravaged for many years, when his eye grew dim and his arm grew weak, lay down to die. And it was precisely then that in addition to this internal feebleness there came upon them from the forests of the North, the sword, and thus there was literally fulfilled the terms of this passage. The sword of the barbarian was added to her own blinded and palsied weakness, and thus judgment inflicted in exact accordance with the words of this prophecy. God often uses instruments, which he afterwards throws into the fire.

PRACTICAL INFERENCES.

(1.) No defence shall protect the wicked from punishment, when God's time has come. Though they tower as high and strong as Lebanon, the storm shall bow their summits, and though they hide themselves as deep as the lairs in the creeping thickets of Jordan, the tempest shall find them out, and wrap them in ruin, (v. 1—3.)

(2.) Sin is always folly, and the sinner always a fool, for he secures the great evil of punishment in exchange for the small good of gratification, and therefore always makes a fool's bargain, (v. 4, 5.)

(3.) Wicked rulers are a curse of God on a wicked nation. Now as religion tends to prevent such rulers, or at least prevent their choice, there is an obvious connection between politics and religion. Church and state may and ought to be separated ; politics and religion ought not, for thus the state becomes exposed to the curse of God, and political evil follows in the train of moral evil, (v. 6.)

(4.) Blessed are the poor in spirit, for theirs is the Kingdom of Heaven, (v. 7.)

(5.) Union of feeling in a people is a mark of the favor of God, and disunion a token of his wrath, and usually a beginning of the downfall of a people. May this token of God's wrath long be averted from the people of these United States! (v. 7.)

(6.) Christ cannot be rejected with impunity. Even the Jews, who " did it ignorantly in unbelief," paid a terrible penalty for their crime ; how much more terrible will be the punishment of those who have all their unbelief, without any of their ignorance, (v. 8—11.)

(7.) Men now sometimes reject Christ for a far less

reward than thirty pieces of silver, and of course with far more guilt than Judas, (v. 12, 13.)

(8.) God may bear long with the wicked, but there is a point where the piling avalanche will cease to be held back, and descend in fearful ruin, (v. 14—17.)

VII. Future Blessings to Judah.

Chapter 12 : 1—9.

ANALYSIS.

I. A message of wrath to the enemies of Israel, (v. 1.)

II. God will use the Jewish people, or the Theocracy, as instruments of wrath against his enemies and theirs, (v. 2—4.)

III. A regularly organized government shall exist, which shall protect the people, (v. 5, 6.)

IV. In scenes of peril and trouble God will protect his people, but to prevent the city from looking contemptuously on the country, the former will be rescued by the latter, (v. 7—9.)

THIS chapter ushers in a set of facts over which there hangs some obscurity, both as to the persons to whom they refer and the time of their fulfilment. They are placed subsequent to the rejection of Christ, and yet they seem to refer to a time yet future, and to represent the rejection of Christ as not a hopeless alienation from God. There can be but little doubt that the events here predicted are yet future. The persons referred to are, we believe, the people of God, the New Testament succession of the Theocracy, the Church of Jesus Christ, which is the continuation of the kingdom

1 The burden of the word of the LORD for Israel, saith the LORD, which stretcheth forth the heavens, and lay- eth the foundation of the earth, and formeth the spirit of man within him.

of God as it existed in the Jewish economy. This brings this prophecy in harmony with the rest of the book, which is designed to trace out the historic course of the covenant people down to the time when the unbelieving Jewish element was to be eliminated, and onward to the period when it should be restored in penitence and faith to the one living Church of the living God.

Henderson supposes that this prophecy refers to the restored Jews, in their national capacity, but this is too narrow an object to contain its promises. Calvin takes essentially the view already presented, and considers these promises made to the whole Church of the future, including the restored Jews, though made in terms taken from the existing and past form of the Church.

V. 1. "A Burden. The word of Jehovah upon Israel, saith Jehovah, who stretches the heavens, and establishes the earth, and forms the spirit of man within him."

V. 1. The word " Burden " is usually, if not always, prefixed as a title to threatening prophecies, as if to indicate the weight of wrath that they embosomed in their dark clouds. Although the drift of this prophecy is consoling, yet it is not wholly so, for the greater part of its predictions are threatenings of evil to the enemies of the chosen people. The words " upon Israel " are supposed by Hengstenberg to indicate Israel as the object of the threatening predictions that follow. Israel, or the ten tribes, being taken as typical of the enemies of the chosen people. This view is favored by the fact that all the subsequent promises are made to Judah and Jerusalem, and none to Israel. It is however not at all an obvious or usual sense of the word Israel, though the sense thus expressed is the real object of the prophecy, *viz.*, comfort to the people of God by the assurance that their enemies should all be destroyed. As there is really no necessity for adopting so unusual a sense to explain the word "burden," it is useless to adopt it.

The language describing God's attributes here is peculiar. It is not who *hath* stretched the heavens, &c., but who is *now* stretching them, and, by a ceaseless exertion of his power, upholding the great ongoings of the universe. The Bible is ignorant of that philosophy which teaches that God has created the universe and wound up its machinery like a clock, and then left it to run on by its own inherent energies. From moment to moment he is exerting his power in maintaining the movements of visible things. The argument is that God is doing all these mighty works, and hence will be able to do less mighty, and that as he has not excluded himself from his creation, he is able to do all that he has promised. It is therefore a most fitting introduction.

V. 2. "Behold! I make Jerusalem a threshold of shaking to all nations round about, and also upon Judah shall it be, in the siege against Jerusalem."

2 Behold, I will make Jerusalem a cup of trembling unto all the people round about, when they shall be in the siege both against Judah *and* against Jerusalem.

3 ¶ And in that day will I make Jerusalem a burdensome stone for all people : all that burden themselves with it shall be cut in pieces, though all the people of the earth be gathered together against it.

V. 2. The word סַף is usually translated cup, but the more common, if not the only proper meaning, is "threshold," and as the same figure essentially is used in v. 3, it is most appropriate here. The meaning is that when the nations assail Jerusalem they shall find a crash of ruin falling upon them, just like the man who on entering the house finds the threshold to give way under his feet, bringing down the building in ruins upon his head. The phrase "upon Judah shall it be," &c., is a difficult one, but seems to mean that Judah shall be involved in the evils of the siege against Jerusalem, *i. e.*, that the evil shall be general, so that all, even the most remote, shall feel it.

V. 3. " And it shall be in that day, I will make Jerusalem a stone of burden to all the nations, all who lift it up shall surely gash themselves, and there shall be gathered against her all people of the earth."

V. 3 declares that the efforts of the enemies of the Church to overthrow her shall be futile and injurious only to themselves. It shall be like some huge rock, the efforts to raise which only wound and bruise the hand of him who makes the attempt. Jerome states that it was a custom among the cities of Palestine to have a large rock, the lifting of which was a test of strength, and that he himself saw in the Acropolis at

4 In that day, saith the LORD, I will smite every horse with astonishment, and his rider with madness : and I will open mine eyes upon the house of Judah, and will smite every horse of the people with blindness.

Athens a huge sphere of brass, which was used for the same purpose ; no athlete being allowed to enter the games who was unable to lift it. Jerusalem has literally been such a stone, and the Church of God pre-eminently has been a test of this kind, to all who have attempted to use her for selfish purposes.

V. 4. "In that day, saith Jehovah, I will smite every horse with affright, and his rider with madness, and upon the house of Judah will I open my eyes, and every horse of the nations will I smite with blindness."

V. 4 drops this metaphor, and as cavalry was in ancient warfare a very important arm of attack, and one which the Jewish people feared, God promises so to confound the horse and his rider as to prevent them from doing any injury to the chosen people, to whom under· the phrase, "I will open my eyes," the supervision and protection of God is promised. He had seemed to slumber or to close his eyes upon and forget them, but now he will bestow upon them special attention and protection. A distinction is evidently made between Judah and Jerusalem, or the province and the metropolis, but what is the exact fact alluded to by this distinction, in the future, we cannot tell. It implies a difference of privilege and of strength among the people of God, corresponding to the difference between a residence within the fortified walls of the city and the hallowed

N

5 And the governors of Judah shall say in their heart, The inhabitants of Jerusalem *shall be* my strength in the LORD of hosts their God.

6 ¶ In that day will I make the governors of Judah like an hearth of fire among the wood, and like a torch of fire in a sheaf; and they shall devour

shadow of the temple, and a residence in the less holy and less secure regions of the country.

V. 5. "And the princes of Judah say in their hearts, my strength (*is*) the inhabitants of Jerusalem, in Jehovah of Hosts, their God."

V. 5 brings out this distinction more emphatically. There are several grammatical difficulties about this verse, but the most natural course seems to be to take אֶמְצָה as a noun meaning strength in apposition with "inhabitants of Jerusalem," and "in Jehovah" as explanatory of the connection asserted by this apposition. The meaning then would be, that the princes of Judah (who speak for the people) recognize Jerusalem, which is the place of God's special manifestation, as the source from which their strength is to come, and yet as only the medium of transmission, the strength itself residing at last only in Jehovah. The general fact predicted seems to be that cordial union of all portions of the Church from the lowest to the highest, that will give the fullest scope for the exertion of God's power in delivering and blessing his people.

V. 6. "In that day I will make the princes of Judah as a pan of fire among faggots, and as a torch of fire in a sheaf, and they shall consume on the right hand and on the left all the nations round about, and Jerusalem shall yet sit in her own place in Jerusalem."

V. 6 intimates, that because of the meek acknowledg-

all the people round about, on the right hand and on the left : and Jerusalem shall be inhabited again in her own place, *even* in Jerusalem.

7 The Lord also shall save the tents of Judah first, that the glory of the house of David and the glory of the inhabitants of Jerusalem do not magnify *themselves* against Judah.

ment of subordination made by the province, they who humbled themselves shall be exalted, and the province should be made the instrument of delivering the metropolis, and should consume the enemies assembled against the church as a pan of coals sets fire to a pile of dry faggots, or a torch consumes a sheaf of straw. Jerusalem sitting " in her own place," describes a settled and secure state of things in the Church, which should be brought about by the agency of these feebler and humbler instrumentalities, the princes of Judah.

V. 7. "And Jehovah shall help the tents of Judah first, that the glory of the House of David, and the glory of the inhabitant of Jerusalem, may not be magnified over Judah."

V. 7 assigns the reason for the preference given to the humbler agencies ; it is to prevent all swelling of pride, and show that God and not man is the source of this deliverance, and also to prevent the more favored from looking down contemptuously on the less favored. The " tents of Judah," in their insecurity and lowliness are placed in contrast with the lofty mountains of Jerusalem. As these privileges were likely to produce pride, God would bestow the honor of this deliverance, as well as the first possession of it, on those who were less favored externally than the inhabitants of the holy city. Such has been his plan in the past, and such it is here declared it will be in the great struggles of the future ; the weak

8 In that day shall the Lord defend the inhabitants of Jerusalem; and he that is feeble among them at that day shall be as David; and the house of things shall confound the mighty, and the things that are not bring to naught things that are, in order that no flesh may glory in his presence.

V. 8. "In that day Jehovah will protect the dweller in Jerusalem, and the feeble among them in that day shall be as David, and the house of David as God, as the angel of Jehovah before them."

V. 8 declares that this favor shall not be restricted to the lowly and less favored, lest it might generate the very evil it was designed to avoid, but that all portions of the Church should be visited and blessed. The highest earthly type of might and glory to the Jew was David, and the highest heavenly was the Jehovah angel, the divine messenger who led them through the desert. These are taken as the standards of comparison to describe this future glory. The weakest of the future shall be equal to the strongest of the past, whilst the strong ("the house of David") shall be as God, namely as the angel of Jehovah. There is no reason for taking *elohim* in any other than its usual sense, expressing the abstract notion of Deity, whilst *Jehovah*, and especially "the angel of *Jehovah*," expresses that concrete and manifested form of divinity that was most significant to the Jew. The apposition here is another proof that the angel of the covenant is a divine person.

V. 9. "And it shall be in that day I will seek to destroy all nations who come up against Jerusalem."

V. 9 declares in general terms the destruction of all

David *shall be* as God, as the angel of the LORD before them.

9 ¶ And it shall come to pass in that day, *that* I will seek to destroy all the nations that come against Jerusalem.

the enemies that shall combine against the Church, here symbolised by Jerusalem.

As the events predicted here are yet future, it were unwise to dogmatise in regard to their exact nature. The general meaning seems to be, that there shall be hereafter a wide and formidable combination of enemies against the Church ; that God shall deliver her, not by the instruments to which she has looked, but by others, of the humbler and obscurer part ; and that this deliverance should be accompanied by cordial union of affection among all portions of the Church, and followed by a vast accession of strength to every portion of it, and by complete overthrow of her enemies. This great struggle yet before the Church, is one that seems to have loomed up like the lurid smoke of some distant battle to the eye of all the prophets, from Enoch to the seer of the Apocalypse. Blessed is he who is then found faithful !

There is however another great event that is to accompany this mighty struggle, which is, the conversion and restoration of the Jewish people to the Church from which they have been so long separated. This is alluded to and implied in the remaining verses of this chapter and the opening verses of the succeeding.

PRACTICAL INFERENCES.

(1.) The agency of God is still exerted as really in the

continued existence of the universe, as in its original creation, (v. 1.)

(2.) The ark of God may be allowed, on account of the sins of his Church to fall into the hands of the Philistines, but it shall be a booty of fearful import, and one, which, over mutilated and prostrate Dagons, shall at last be restored to its rightful possessors, (v. 2, 3.)

(3.) The promise of God is the best protection of his Church, in the time of peril, (v. 4, 5.)

(4.) God may seem to forget his people in their trouble, but it will only be a seeming oblivion, for at the proper time he will open his eyes upon them, and show them that he slumbers not nor sleeps, (v. 4.)

(5.) However feeble the cause of religion may be now, there is a time coming when it shall be in fact what it is in right, and in actual result what it is in natural tendency, the mightiest element in human things, (v. 6, 8.)

(6.) The whole plan of God's dealings with man is to humble that pride, the root of which is selfishness, and the fruit of which is every form of sin, (v. 7.)

(7.) The enemies of the Church of God shall at last perish, (v. 9.)

10 And I will pour upon the house of David, and upon the inhabitants of Jerusalem, the spirit of grace and of supplications: and they shall look

---

VIII. Future Repentance and Blessing to Jerusa-lem.

Chapter 12 : 10—*end*.

ANALYSIS.

I. The outpouring of the spirit on the Church, which shall then contain the restored Jews, (v. 10.)

II. The penitence that shall exist because of their former treatment of Christ. (1) Deep, (v. 11.)　(2) Pervading.　(3) Personal, (v. 12—14.)

V. 10. " And I pour out upon the house of David, and upon the inhabitants of Jerusalem, a spirit of grace and of supplication, and they look upon me, whom they pierced, and they lament for him, as the lamenting of an only child, and they mourn for him as the mourning of a first-born."

V. 10. There is here predicted a great spiritual blessing from God on the Church, but contemplated mainly as now containing the penitent Jews. " A spirit of grace and supplication " is an outpouring of the spirit of God, that awakens gracious affections and leads the heart to prayer. The spirit of prayer is the gauge of the spirit of grace, and the mercury whose rise or fall is an unerring test of the state of the Church.

In this mighty revival that shall take place in the future, there will be much prayer and much penitence. This penitence shall pervade the whole Church, but especial prominence is given here to the recovered Jews.

upon me whom they have pierced, and | in bitterness for him, as one that is in
they shall mourn for him, as one | bitterness for *his* first-born.
mourneth for *his* only *son*, and shall be

" They shall look on me whom they have pierced." As
God is here the speaker, this passage has always been a
stumbling-block to the Jews, for how could God be
pierced? The only fact that explains it is that which
they have not yet admitted, that they have crucified and
slain that prince of peace who was God manifest in the
flesh. As soon as they admit this fact they will see the
consistency of the passage, and will mourn the guilt of
their fathers in crucifying the incarnate Son, and their
own guilt in so long rejecting him.

John 19 : 37 refers this passage to the piercing of
Christ's side, but as this was the act of a Roman soldier
and not of the Jewish people, it must be regarded as
only a partial fulfilment of the prophecy. It refers to
all the sufferings of Christ, which culminated in his
death on the cross, and affirms that then the Jews will
admit what heretofore they have rejected, a suffering
and dying Messiah. There is a change of person from
the first to the third, which is not unusual with the
prophets, (see Nordheimer's Grammar, § 768, 1, 6,)
and which, in view of what was to be said in reference
to the speaker, was highly appropriate.

This passage has always been regarded as one of no
small difficulty ; at least, the expositors have found no
small difficulty with it, from the fact that if its obvious
meaning be admitted, a real prophecy and a suffering

and yet divine Messiah must also be admitted.   Hence
Jews in earlier times, and neologists in later, have
endeavored to get rid of this meaning.   Some alleged
that רָקַר here means not to pierce, but to grieve, or to
insult, and that the charge is that of insulting or blas-
pheming God.   This is the rendering of the LXX and
the Chaldee.   Calvin favors it to a certain extent, but
finds, in the literal fulfilment on the cross, a divinely
arranged procedure, giving a symbolical exemplification
of this insulting treatment of God.   Rosenmuller,
Eichorn, Theiner, Maurer, De Wette, Winer, and others,
contend very strenuously for this opinion.   But it is a
sufficient objection to it that the word never occurs in
that sense, but always in the sense of literal piercing,
even in this prophecy, (ch. 13 : 3.)   And the whole
context is at variance with this meaning.   The mourning, to which it is compared, was for a literal piercing,
or death, in the case of Josiah, and, unless it is a literal
death here, the depth of sorrow indicated in these words
seems hardly explicable, and the analogy fails.

That the passage refers to Messiah was admitted,
even among the Jews, the later interpreters explaining
it of Messiah Ben Joseph, or the suffering Messiah,
whom they invented to meet the passages of Scripture
that speak so clearly of this characteristic of the promised Redeemer.   But as they believed that this Messiah
son of Joseph was a mere man, the difficulty met them
that Jehovah declared " they shall look on ME whom
they have pierced ;" so that if it refers to the Messiah

he cannot be a mere man, but must be divine. To escape this difficulty, they changed the text, and made it read " him," instead of " me." This was at first only a marginal reading, as appears from some of the MSS., but was afterwards admitted into the text. But many of the most able Jews reject this gloss, and admit that " me " is the true reading. Scarcely any scholar of any note, even among the infidel critics, admits this interpolation. Hence this evasion is utterly inadmissible, and the text still stands, asserting that the Jews would look at Jehovah whom they had slain, a prophecy which can only be interpreted in the light of the cross.

It is useless to discuss the opinion of some of the early Jews, adopted in later times by Jahn, Bauer, Bertholdt, and others, that the mourning here was for the death of Judas Maccabeus, or some other Jewish leader, for this is liable to the same objections with the last-named opinion. Calmet admits this view, but says that Judas Maccabeus was a type of Christ. Ackermann, who quotes it at length, coincides with it as most probable. But there is no necessity for supposing any such reference as this, for the context refers obviously to events later than the Maccabean age, and events some of which are still future. Indeed, this very mourning is obviously yet to take place.

Hence, the only meaning that the text will bear is, that Jehovah is the speaker, and that he is speaking of himself, and the manner in which he has been treated by his people, and will be hereafter. Having, in the

11 In that day shall there be a great ing of Hadadrimmon in the valley of
mourning in Jerusalem, as the mourn- Megiddon.

previous passage, under the symbol of a shepherd,
declared how the people would treat him, in their
blindness and madness, he then predicts that they would
repent of this treatment, and turn to him with deep and
heartrending penitence.

When their eyes were open to see what they had
done, they would mourn. The bitterness of this mourning is described by two illustrations, a private and a
public. The private is the grief that a parent feels at
the loss of a first-born and an only child. The bitterness of this agony in any parent is a most vivid image
of sorrow, but to a Jew, with his passion for posterity,
and his impression of disgrace and curse connected with
childlessness, this illustration was one of the most significant that could be used. There is an allusion to this
passage in Matt. 24 : 30, and also in Rev. 1 : 7, implying its Messianic interpretation.

V. 11. " And in that day the mourning shall be great in Jerusalem, as the mourning of Hadadrimmon in the vale of Megiddo."

V. 11 expresses the public example of sorrow, and it
was the most expressive in the history of the Jewish
people. The death of the good Josiah was the darkest
and saddest event in the history of the monarchy, for it
was the quenching of all hope. He was a link of bright
memories in the past, and bright hopes in the future,
and when he fell, and fell under the displeasure of God,
it was as the giving up of the ghost. It was like the

12 And the land shall mourn, every family apart ; the family of the house of David apart, and their wives apart ; the family of the house of Nathan apart, and their wives apart ;

13 The family of the house of Levi apart, and their wives apart ; the family of Shimei apart, and their wives apart ;

14 All the families that remain, every family apart, and their wives apart.

death of Hampden in the English history, or like what the death of Washington in the darkest hour of the Revolution would have been in our own, a calamity that would have wrung a wail of agony and despair from a whole people.

Hadad Rimmon was the name of a place in the plain of Esdraelon, that great battle-field of nations, near Megiddo, and was called, in the time of Jerome, Maximianopolis. It was probably named from the Syrian god, Rimmon.

V. 12—14. " And the land mourns, family by family apart ; the family of the house of David apart and their wives apart ; the family of the house of Nathan apart and their wives apart ; the family of the house of Levi apart and their wives apart ; the family of the house of Shimei apart and their wives apart ; all the remaining families, family by family apart, and their wives apart."

V. 12—14 describes the universality of this mourning. It should extend to every family, and every individual, leading each one to retire alone and weep. The selection of names seems designed to express the fact, that from the highest to the lowest this mourning should extend. David and Levi express the kingly and priestly orders, or the civil and ecclesiastical, whilst Nathan, who was not the prophet, but a descendant of David, (see 2 Sam. 5 : 14, Luke 3 : 31,) and Shimei, who was a descendant of Levi, (see Numb. 3 : 18, 21,) carry the lamentation to the remotest members of these two great orders.

The mourning of the wives apart simply alludes to the Jewish custom of separating the males from the females, even in acts of worship.

PRACTICAL INFERENCES.

(1.) There shall be a revival of religion in the future history of the Church that shall gather in the Jews, (v. 10.)

(2.) This revival shall be characterized by the invariable marks of an outpouring of the spirit, namely, a spirit of prayer and penitence, (v. 10.)

(3.) Prayer is the barometer of the Church. When the spirit of supplication is low, there is but little of the Spirit of God, and as soon as the prayer meeting begins to fill up with earnest suppliants, the Christian may hope for a blessing, (v. 10.)

(4.) All true repentance arises from a sight of a dying Saviour, one who has died for us. Terror may produce remorse, only a sense of forgiven sin will ever produce true repentance. True repentance is after all only love weeping at the foot of the cross, the soul sorrowing for sins that have been so freely forgiven, (v. 10.)

(5.) True religion is a personal thing, and when it takes strong hold of the heart, will lead the soul apart to solitary wrestling with God, and acts of personal humbling before him. Confession of sins past and re-

1 In that day there shall be a foun-   to the inhabitants of Jerusalem for sin
tain opened to the house of David and   and for uncleanness.

solutions of obedience for time to come.   Grace needs
solitary meditation to grow, just as much as the plant
needs the repose and darkness of night, (v. 12—14.)

IX. FRUITS OF PENITENCE.

CHAPTER 13 : 1—6.

ANALYSIS.

I. The opening of the fountain of pardon and purity, (v. 1.)

II. The extermination of idolatry, false prophecy, and sorcery
from the land, (v. 2.)

III. The zeal of God's people in the work of cleansing, (v. 3,)
and the penitent confessions of false prophets themselves, (v.
4—6.)

V. 1. " In that day there shall be a fountain opened, to the
house of David, and to the inhabitants of Jerusalem, for sin, and
for uncleanness."

WE have shown before that the preceding chapter
refers to a great revival of religion in the Church, which
is yet future, and to this revival especially as it should
include the Jews, who would at that time be restored
to the Church from which they had been so long separated
by unbelief.   The depth of their penitence is described
very vividly in ch. 12 : 8—14.   Connected with this
penitence, however, would then be, what their previous
mourning had never attained, a felt possession of pardon.   This is represented by the metaphor of a fountain,

2 ¶ And it shall come to pass in that day, saith the LORD of hosts, *that* I will cut off the names of the idols out of the land, and they shall no more be remembered : and also I will cause the prophets and the unclean spirits to pass out of the land.

that bestows the double blessing of refreshment to the thirsty and purification to the unclean.   This fountain is not then opened for the first time, for it has long been flowing from the riven rock.   But it is opened then for the first time to the house of David, after their long and weary wanderings.   Like Hagar they had wandered in the wilderness until they were ready to perish, ignorant of the refreshment that was near them, until the Lord opened their eyes to see the fountain. Prominence is here given to its purifying power, because of the guilt that had so long rested on the covenant people.   The word "sin" here refers to the guilt, and "uncleanness" to the defilement of moral evil, and the verse teaches the Jews that mere ceremonial observances are not sufficient to remove these.   The two cardinal doctrines of justification and sanctification by the blood of Christ are therefore here brought out clearly.

V. 2. "And it shall be in that day, saith Jehovah of Hosts, I will cut off the names of the idols from the land, and they shall not be remembered any more ; and also the prophets, and the spirit of uncleanness will I remove from the land."

V. 2 describes the consequences of this pardon.   A free forgiveness does not lead to indolence, but to a more vigorous discharge of duty and extirpation of sin. The two great sins of the Jewish people before the cap-

3 And it shall come to pass, *that* when any shall yet prophesy, then his father and his mother that begat him shall say unto him, Thou shalt not

tivity were idolatry and false prophecy, and these are taken as the types of all ungodliness of whatever specific form. All actual, outward idolatry and false prophecy have ceased among the Jews, and hence these sins are only the types of sin in general. It is, however, worthy of remark, that the only sin of heart that is called emphatically idolatry, is a sin that is supposed to be peculiarly that which besets the Jew, the worship of mammon, and who can tell but that the wealth of the world is gathering into the hands of Jews, in anticipation of that mighty Exodus that is yet to be made by the sons of Jacob. Certain it is that a general conversion of the Jews would throw an amount of wealth into the treasury of the Lord, of which we now can have no conception, and give a blow to the rule of gold such as no other event we can now specify would be likely to do. "The spirit of uncleanness" is here put in contrast with the Spirit of God, who inspired the true prophets, and refers doubtless to more than a mere impersonal depravity of human souls, but to spiritual influences of demoniac form, such as are so often referred to in the Bible in connection with sin.

V. 3. "And it happens, if a man still prophesy, his father and his mother who begat him say unto him, 'Thou shalt not live, because thou hast spoken falsehood in the name of Jehovah,' and his father and his mother who begat him, pierce him through in his prophesying."

V. 3 describes in dramatic form the effect of this re-

live ; for thou speakest lies in the name of the LORD : and his father and his mother that begat him shall thrust him through when he prophesieth.

4 And it shall come to pass in that day, *that* the prophets shall be ashamed every one of his vision, when he hath prophesied ; neither shall they wear a rough garment to deceive :

moval of sin. There is not only a passive abandonment of sin, but also an action antagonistic to it that is strong enough to overcome the most powerful principles of our nature. The one selected is parental affection, whose strength is such as usually to survive the greatest unworthiness in its object. The prodigal boy may be despised and hated by all the world, and yet the heart of the father will yearn kindly toward the hapless out-cast, and the arms of the mother will be ever ready to fold him in forgiving love. Now the love of duty that can surpass an affection like this, must be of a most controlling character. The precise incidents here con-ceived seem to have been suggested by Deut. 13 : 6—10, 18 : 20, where the nearest relation of the false prophet was required to put him to death, a heroic sense of duty that had been embodied thus in Hebrew law, long before Brutus made it famous by a similar act in Roman history. The general truth is, that the religious emo-tions shall swallow up, like Aaron's rod, all others in the nature.

V. 4. "And it happens in that day, the prophets are ashamed from their vision in their prophesying, and they shall no longer put on the mantle of hair to deceive."

V. 4 declares that so general will be the power of this religious reformation, that even sin itself shall hide its head in shame. The false prophets shall be ashamed

o

5 But he shall say, I *am* no prophet, I *am* an husbandman ; for man taught me to keep cattle from my youth.

6 And *one* shall say unto him, What *are* these wounds in thy hands? Then he shall answer, *Those* with which I was wounded *in* the house of my friends.

to utter their pretended visions. The prophets usually wore a hairy garment, such as was worn by mourners, because of the solemn and often mournful purport of their messages. Hence deceivers adopted the same garb, but this symbol of deception shall then be laid aside in dread of the fiery storm of zeal for God that shall sweep the land.

V. 5, 6. "And he says, 'I am not a prophet, I am a husbandman, for a man has sold me from the time of my youth.' And he *(the former)* says unto him, 'What then are these wounds between thy hands?' And he replies : *(they are the wounds)* 'which I received in the house of my lovers.'"

V. 5 and 6 describe in dialogue form the detection of one of these prophets. He is seized by some zealous vindicator of the law, and in his fright he exclaims that he is not a false prophet, but a field servant, who was purchased for that purpose in his youth, and hence could not have exercised the prophetic function, being under the absolute control of a master. The interrogator, however, detects falsehood in the statements of the prophet, and forces him to confess his character. He sees scars in his hands. The phrase "between thy hands," means this, as appears from Prov. 26 : 13, where "between" has the same signification. He demands an explanation of these scars, and the guilty man confesses with shame that they were received in the service of idols. This verse is often applied to Christ, in the grossest misapprehension of its meaning. It applies solely to the detected false prophet. Some have taken the passage as a continuance of his defence, asserting that these were scars received from his master, but besides destroying the fine dramatic finale that the real sense gives us, it is inconsistent with the terms used. "Lovers," in the Hebrew, is the word usually employed to represent the objects of idolatrous love and service, and must so be taken here, and 1 Kings 18 : 28, and other passages show that cutting the flesh was a part often of idolatrous worship It is, therefore, the trembling confession of a confused culprit, who is detected, and in shame and terror acknowledges his crime in hope of mercy.

But it is proper to say that some of the ablest interpreters prefer the other interpretation, which represents the scars as received from his parents, among whom are Calvin, Hitzig, Maurer, Ackermann, and some of the older expositors. Hengstenberg, Henderson, and others prefer the one just given, making the passage to be a highly picturesque description of the zeal for God, the hatred of evil, and the shrinking fear and concealment of sin that will be found in the great Revival of the future.

PRACTICAL INFERENCES.

(1.) The fountain of pardon and purity is flowing beside many a soul that is too blind to perceive it, (v. 1.)

(2.) The atoning work of Christ has provided for

purity as well as pardon, and the one is inseparable from the other. Ignorance or malignity must be the origin of the averment that justification by faith is not favorable to sanctification, (v. 1, 2.)

(3.) Love to God must be paramount to all other affections, even the tenderest of which the heart is capable. It is, in our present imperfect sanctification, inconceivable to us how we could acquiesce in the perdition of our children, without a pang that would poison all the bliss of heaven, and yet it shall be so. Much as we love them, we shall love God and his law immeasurably more, (v. 3.)

(4.) Sinners shall at last be made to confess their sins, and the justice of their punishment, and the bitterest drop in the cup of their agony will be that they have wrung it out for themselves, and that it is all just, (v. 4—6.)

X. THE SWORD AWAKING AGAINST THE SHEPHERD.

CHAPTER 13 : 7—9.

ANALYSIS.

I. The Divine decree, that Christ should die for the sins of his people, (v. 7.)

II. The dismay and dispersion that his death would occasion, (v. 7, 8.)

III. The salvation of the elect through much tribulation, (v. 9.)

IT is not unusual with the prophets to give at the opening or the close of a prophecy a summary of its

contents.   An instance of the first, we have in ch. 11 :
1–3, and an instance of the second we have in the passage before us.   It sums up the preceding prophecy,
which had declared the assumption of the pastoral charge
of the flock by the Messiah, his rejection by the people,
their rejection by God, their dispersion and subsequent
restoration.   This summary is in this case the more necessary, because the reason for cutting off the Messiah
was not stated.   Only the human agency was brought
out, because the deeper significance of this awful fact
was not pertinent to the scope of that portion of the
prophecy.   It seemed a mysterious thing that one whose
coming was to be such a blessing should be cut off before he had bestowed that blessing.   It seemed a final
triumph of wickedness, and a defeat of the merciful purposes of God by the insane folly of man.   It was therefore necessary before ending the prophecy to bring to
view that deeper mystery that underlaid this fact, and
show that God's great purposes were in it all, and that
what seemed man's final ruin was really man's appointed
salvation.

The meaning of this passage is clearly fixed by Christ,
when in Matt. 26 : 31, 32, he applies it expressly to himself, at that dread hour when he was about to finish the
mystery of redemption.   There is in the whole compass
of human knowledge, nothing more awfully sublime,
than this seeming schism in the Godhead.   It is as if sin
was so dreadful an evil, that the assumption of its guilt
by a sinless Mediator must for a time make a division

7 ¶ Awake, O sword against my smite the Shepherd, and the sheep Shepherd, and against the man *that is* shall be scattered: and I will turn my fellow, saith the LORD of hosts: mine hand upon the little ones.

even in the absolute unity of the Godhead itself. It is the most awful illustration of the repulsive and separating power of sin, that the history of the universe affords.

V. 7. "O sword! awake against my shepherd, against a man, my nearest kin, saith Jehovah of Hosts, smite the shepherd, and the sheep shall be scattered, and I will bring back my hand upon the little ones."

This verse has been variously interpreted. Calvin thinks that it applies to Christ only in common with the whole body of pastors, and cannot be restricted to him or to his death. Maurer refers it to Jehoiakim, others to Pekah, others to Judas Maccabeus, and others to the false prophets of v. 4—6. But as Sanctius well remarks, we have this verse expounded by the very best expositor, Jesus Christ, and applied specifically to himself, in Matt. 26 : 31. The obvious connection of this verse with ch. 11 : 4—14, would corroborate this exposition, were it necessary to add to the authority of the omniscient prophet.

The sword is the symbol of judicial power. The taking away of life being the highest function of government, the sword, which is the instrument of violent death, was selected as the symbol of these functions. The magistrate was called one who beareth the sword, see Rom. 13 : 4, because he wielded judicial power. Hence the great doctrine here set forth is, that the death of Christ was a judicial act, in which he endured the penalty of that law whose penal power was symbolised by this sword of divine wrath. The sheep had deserved the blow, but the shepherd bares his own bosom to the sword, and is wounded for the sins of his people, and bears those sins in his own body on the tree. The vicarious nature of the atonement is therefore distinctly involved in this passage.

But who was this shepherd? " A man, my nearest kin." He was a man, with all human sympathies and emotions, but he was more than a man, the nearest kin of Jehovah. The word עֲמִית is only found elsewhere in the Pentateuch, where it is used for the nearest kin, and sometimes as synonymous with brother. See Lev. 5 : 17, etc. It is never used to indicate similarity of office, as Socinians assert on this passage, but always nearness of relation or kindred. Hence it here must refer to a human nature that beyond this humanity has a nature in the nearest possible relation to Jehovah, which of course must be a divine nature. Hence we have here clearly a twofold nature in the suffering Messiah, human and divine.

The versions vary in rendering this phrase.

The LXX renders it, " a man, my fellow-citizen ;" Aquila, " a man, my kinsman ;" Symmachus, " a man of my people ;" Theodotian, " a man, my neighbor ;" the Syriac, " the man, my friend ;" the Vulgate, " a man, my connection ;" De Wette, " the man, my equal ;" Arnheim, " the man whom I have associated with myself." The last two versions are remarkable, as coming

8 And it shall come to pass, *that* in all the land, saith the LORD, two parts therein shall be cut off *and* die ; but the third shall be left therein.

the one from a Rationalist and the other from a Jew, and express very nearly the exact truth. It is one equal with God, and associated with him, and such an one can only be found in Immanuel.

The scattering of the sheep must not be limited exclusively to the dispersion of the disciples on the night of Christ's arrest, but refers to that general dispersion that should follow the death of Messiah. The flock that the shepherd was to feed was the whole theocratic people, of whom the Christians were but a part. The dispersion, therefore, applies to the whole people. The extent of the dispersion is explained in the next verses. To "bring back the hand" is to interpose in reference to any one, whatever be the animus of the interposition, and to do so upon the little ones, is that interposition in favor of the humble and faithful that is alluded to elsewhere, (see ch. 11 : 7, 11.) It was partly fulfilled in the gathering of Jewish disciples into the Christian church.

V. 8. "And it shall be in all the land, saith Jehovah, two portions shall be cut off and die, and the third portion shall remain in it."

V. 8 predicts the destruction of a majority of the theocratic people, after the death of Messiah. The phrase, " a mouth of two," (probably a mouth-portion of two, a double portion of eatables,) is taken from Deut. 21 : 7, and here means a large portion. This

9 And I will bring the third part through the fire, and will refine them as silver is refined, and will try them as gold is tried; they shall call on my name, and I will hear them; I will say, It *is* my people; and they shall say, The LORD *is* my God.

was fulfilled in the immense destruction of the Jewish people that took place after the death of Christ, when probably two-thirds of the nation were destroyed by war, pestilence, and famine.

V. 9. "And I bring the third part into the fire and purify them as silver is purified, and try them as gold is tried. They shall call upon my name, and I will hear them, I will say they are my people, and they shall say, Jehovah is my God."

V. 9 declares that the smaller portion that would be saved, must be brought through great trials. This portion includes not only the Jews who were converted to Christianity, and who passed through the fires of persecution, but also that portion that survived the dispersion, and still remain in unbelief. They are still in the furnace, but the time comes when they shall be purified and return to God in covenant love, and be received by him again into favor. These verses, therefore, give us an epitomised history of redemption, and show that there are yet purposes of mercy in reserve for the ancient covenant people.

PRACTICAL INFERENCES.

(1.) How fearful an evil is sin, when it could call forth the sword against God's own co-equal and well-beloved Son! (v. 7.)

(2.) Christ was man, and yet equal with God, (Phil. 2 : 6,) or, God and man in one person, (v. 7.)

(3.) The death of Christ was the judicial sentence of God against sin, the endurance of the penalty of the law, and was, therefore, strictly vicarious and propitiatory, (v. 7.)

(4.) No human merit can mingle with the infinite merit of the work of Christ, for he trode the wine-press *alone.* It is impossible for us to eke out our works with Christ's work, or to attempt with our "filthy rags" to patch the seamless robe of his righteousness. When the shepherd was smitten the sheep were scattered, and the blow fell on him alone, (v. 7.)

(5.) God often makes his people pass through the furnace, not that they may perish, but that they may be purified, and thus reach a better salvation, (v. 9.)

XI. FUTURE STRUGGLES AND TRIUMPHS OF THE CHURCH.

CHAPTER 14.

ANALYSIS.

I. Great assault on the people of God, (v. 1, 2.)

II. Interposition of God in their favor, (v. 3,) giving them some remarkable means of escape, (v. 4, 5 ;) and after a mingled condition of things, a final and glorious deliverance, (v. 6, 7.)

III. Spiritual blessings and enlargement : (1) a perennial source of spiritual refreshment, (v. 8 ;) (2) the true God the only object of worship throughout the world, (v. 9 ;) (3) special facilities for intercourse among the people of God, (v. 10, 11.)

IV. Judgments on the enemies of God and his people, (v. 12—15 ;) submission of all nations to God's laws, under heavy penalties, (v. 16—19.)

V. Universal holiness, (v. 20, 21.)

THIS chapter is one of those portions of Scripture which, like sealed orders to a vessel, which are not to be opened until a certain latitude is reached, can only be read in perfect comprehension after the Church has reached a point in her history yet future.   Until the seal is removed at the appointed time, we can only conjecture the full meaning of the predictions, and await the clearer light of the future.   The chapter seems to refer to facts distinct from those predicted in the last chapter, probably the last great events of the present dispensation, that are described in other prophecies in terms of such fearful grandeur.   It seems to point to that last great struggle of the powers of evil with the Church, which is to be ended by the coming of Christ in great power, and the complete establishment of his kingdom of glory.   It is therefore parallel with the prediction of Enoch, concerning the coming of the Lord with ten thousand of his holy ones ; with that of Ezek. 39, about the battle of Gog and Magog, and the corresponding passage in Rev. 20, referring to the same great events.   The general facts predicted are, a wide combination against the Church, a time of trouble ensuing, in the midst of which the Lord appears in terrible power, destroys the enemies of his people, establishes the Church in permanent glory, inflicts enduring punishment on the finally wicked, and brings about a state of holiness that shall be the last and perfected state of the Church.

This chapter has been variously interpreted by expo-

1 Behold, the day of the LORD cometh, and thy spoil shall be divided in the midst of thee.

2 For I will gather all nations against Jerusalem to battle; and the city shall be taken, and the houses rifled, and

sitors. Calvin, Grotius, Dathius, Ackermann, and others refer it to the times of the Maccabees. The early interpreters, such as Jerome, Cyril, and Theodoret, and among the later, Lowth, Scott, Adam Clarke, and Henderson apply the first part to the destruction of Jerusalem by Titus, and the rest to events yet future. It is evident that no events have yet occurred in history to which these predictions are applicable without much forcing, and it seems most natural to interpret the first verses of the chapter as we interpret the rest.

V. 1. "Behold a day comes to Jehovah. And thy spoil is divided in the midst of thee."

The phrase "a day comes to Jehovah," means more than that the day of Jehovah comes. It conveys the thought that this time is to be one of special glory to Jehovah, in which his government shall be vindicated and his name glorified. The second member of the verse is addressed to the Church, and shows that she also shall share in the glory of this day. The promise, "thy spoil shall be divided in the midst of thee," is a promise of victory and security. Victory is indicated by "spoil," and security by the manner in which the spoil was to be divided; not secretly in places of concealment, for fear of a return of the enemy, but openly in the midst of the city; showing that the enemy is completely vanquished. Hence this verse is the caption of the prophecy, showing that it predicts glory to

the women ravished ; and half of the city shall go forth into captivity, and the residue of the people shall not be cut off from the city.

3 Then shall the LORD go forth, and fight against those nations, as when he fought in the day of battle.

God and triumph to his Church, taking Jerusalem here as the symbol of the Theocracy, or the Church of the future.

V. 2. "And I collect all the nations against Jerusalem to battle, and the city is taken, and the houses plundered, and the women dishonored, and half the city go forth into captivity, and the remnant of the city shall not be cut off from the city."

V. 2 explains how this spoil comes to be in the hands of the Church. It is the spoil of those who have come up to destroy her. In consequence of her coldness and defections, a combination of enemies is allowed against her. This is represented under the image of a siege, with obvious allusion to the capture of Jerusalem by Babylon. There is first the investiture of the city by the besiegers, then the breach, and then the pillage, brutality, and cruelty that accompanied the sack of a city. But this capture should not be like the first one, so vividly in their memory then, for " the remnant of the city shall not be cut off from the city." There shall be a faithful few who shall be left like wheat when the chaff has been winnowed by the tempest, and who shall not be cut off from the city.

V. 3. "And Jehovah goes forth, and fights against those heathen, as in the day of conflict, in the day of battle."

When the scene is darkest, and the enemies of the Church seem to be completely victorious, God himself appears in a form of terrible majesty, and takes part

4 ¶ And his feet shall stand in that day upon the mount of Olives, which *is* before Jerusalem on the east, and the mount of Olives shall cleave in the midst thereof toward the east and toward the west, *and there shall be* a very great valley ; and half of the mountain shall remove toward the north, and half of it toward the south.

against the invading nations. What shall be the exact mode of this interposition, the event only can fully declare. "The day of conflict," alluded to in the second member of the verse, is probably the Egyptian deliverance, which is called a battle in Ex. 14 : 14, 15 : 3, and which always was regarded as *the* deliverance of the nation, by way of eminence.

V. 4. "And his feet shall stand in that day on the mount of Olives, which is before Jerusalem, on the east, and the mount of Olives is split in the midst from east to west, a great valley, and half the mountain recedes to the north, and half to the south."

V. 4 describes the first great act of interposition, viz., an earthquake, which divides the Mount of Olives in half, and opens out a valley toward the Jordan, which would be a prolongation eastward of the valley of Jehoshaphat. The mount of Olives is chosen as the spot that commanded the finest view of Jerusalem, and hence the one most suitable for God to occupy as a position of observation.

V. 5. "And ye flee into my mountain valley, for the mountain valley will extend to Azal, and ye shall flee, as ye fled before the earthquake, in the days of Uzziah, king of Judah, and there comes Jehovah my God, all holy ones with thee."

V. 5 explains the reason for opening out this valley. The Mount of Olives would be an obstacle in the way of a sudden flight from the city. When, therefore, the earthquake was sent in judgment on the enemies of the

5 And ye shall flee *to* the valley of the mountains; for the valley of the mountains shall reach unto Azal: yea, ye shall flee, like as ye fled from be-

Church, it was necessary that the few faithful should be enabled to escape like Lot from Sodom ; and to enable them to do so in the speediest manner, the same mighty convulsion that was sent to swallow up the enemy opened up a way of escape for them. " My mountain-valley," (lit. valley of my mountains,) would seem to be the valley of Jehoshaphat, which lay along Zion and Moriah, which may be called God's mountains, from their peculiar sacredness. This is said to extend, in consequence of the disruption of the Mount of Olives, to Azal. The word *Azal* means, probably, standing still, or ceasing, and may be used to express the fact that the valley of deliverance should extend to the point where all danger would cease. If it designates any actually existing place, it must have been some small city east of Jerusalem. . . . The earthquake in the days of Uzziah is not mentioned in the historical books of the Old Testament, but is alluded to in Amos 1 : 1, as a very memorable event in the history of Judah. . . . It is impossible for us to take this whole passage literally, for God cannot literally place his feet on the Mount of Olives, but how far it must be taken as figurative, we cannot now tell. It is clear, however, that it predicts scenes of confusion and terror, in the midst of which God shall interpose by some amazing acts, which shall at the same time destroy his enemies and deliver his people. How far the mighty agencies of the material

fore the earthquake in the days of   my God shall come, *and* all the saints
Uzziah king of Judah: and the LORD   with thee.

world shall be actually employed, it is impossible for us
now to say with certainty.

The last member of the verse seems like a sudden exclamation.   After looking at the earthquake, and the
rending mountain, and the flying crowds rushing to a
place of safety, the prophet looks up and sees a sight
that causes him suddenly to cry out with joyful surprise,
"there comes Jehovah my God! all holy ones with
thee!"   The surprise is indicated not only by the ab-
rupt transition, but also by the change of persons from
the third to the second.   The "holy ones" are the inhabitants of heaven, whether angels or redeemed souls,
and the same with the saints, &c., that are so frequently
mentioned in connection with the coming of the Lord.
This coming of Jehovah is distinct from the interposition predicted in v. 3, 4, and seems to be that last great
coming to judgment, elsewhere so vividly depicted.
This exclamation is thrown in parenthetically, like that
in 13 : 7, "awake, O sword," &c., as if the prophet had
lifted his eyes from the dim and troubled scenes he was
contemplating to a more distant but more radiant future, the light of which enabled him to look more
steadily on the scenes more immediately before him.
Having gazed for an instant of exulting rapture on that
glorious procession that he saw approaching, he then
returns in the next verse to describe more in detail the
events he had been just before describing.   This sud-

6 And it shall come to pass in that day, *that* the light shall not be clear, *nor* dark :

den transition from a nearer to a remoter future, that has some connection with it, we have already noticed frequently in this prophecy, and need not pause to explain or defend it, for it is the natural action of the mind in looking at a series of future events.

V. 6. "And it shall be in that day, it shall not be light, precious things are obscured."

This verse returns to the events that are to attend this interposition of God for his Church. The words יְקָרוֹת יִקְפָּאוּן are somewhat obscure, and have received various interpretations. The older versions and some of the modern interpreters, render it " cold and ice." But this is wholly at variance with the usage of at least the second word, which elsewhere means invariably something costly, or precious. Henderson connects " light" with " precious things," and translates it " there shall not be the light of the precious orbs, but condensed darkness." This, however, requires several changes of the reading, and takes the last word as a noun, when it never elsewhere appears in that form. Hengstenberg renders them " that which is precious will become mean," and also refers them to the heavenly bodies. But there is no necessity for such a restriction. יָקָר means anything *costly*, and does not at all suggest the heavenly bodies, if indeed it is applicable to them. And קפָא means *to contract* or *lessen*, and if the received reading be retained, it is the future Kal, and may be construed

P

7 But it shall be one day which shall   night : but it shall come to pass, *that*
be known to the Lord, not day, nor   at evening time it shall be light.

with יְקָרוֹת without any grammatical difficulty, as Hengstenberg has shown. Hence the phrase would mean that
bright things were losing their brightness, and thus their
value. These bright things need not be limited to any
single class of objects.

When the light disappears, all precious things, heavenly and earthly must be obscured, and the general fact
predicted seems to be, that in the time of trouble here declared, all that is most prized among men, all the guiding
lights of human ambition, and all the precious things of
human affection, shall lose their former value, and darken
under a gloomy eclipse.

V. 7. "And it shall be one day, it shall be known to Jehovah,
not day, and not night, and it shall be that in the evening time it
shall be light."

V. 7, declares that this state of darkness shall not be
long in duration, nor shall it be total in its obscurity. It
shall be only " one day, known to Jehovah," but a short
time, and this time limited by the purposes of God. The
words, "not day, not night," indicate that it shall not
be a total obscurity, but only a twilight dimness, in
which the darkness of the past shall be yielding to the
light of the future. And then when it seems to the
fainting hope of God's people that this darkness is thick-
ening into the deeper gloom of night, it suddenly breaks
away, like the outburst of the setting sun, after a day
of clouds, and at " evening time it shall be light." The

8 And it shall be in that day, *that* living waters shall go out from Jerusalem ; half of them toward the former sea, and half of them toward the hinder sea : in summer and in winter shall it be.

meaning is as obvious as the image is beautiful, and in the experience of many a Christian has it been true, as it will be in the great sunset of the world, that when the gloom that has thickened through the waning noon seems to be deepening into the blackness of night, then is the sudden sunburst of a bright revealing of the face of God, so that in the evening time there is light.

Henderson translates this verse, " when it shall not be day and night," and interprets it to mean that it shall be all day and no night, and refers it to the Millenium. But this wrenches the verse from its context, and gives no sufficient force to the last clause, " in the evening time it shall be light." This implies that previous to the evening it had not been clear light, and naturally refers to the nearest subject.

V. 8. " And it shall be in that day, living waters shall go out from Jerusalem, their half to the eastern sea, and their half to the western sea, in summer and winter it shall be."

V. 8 predicts the coming of blessings on the earth, by means of the Church. These blessings are set forth under the symbol of living (*i. e.* running) waters, a symbol which is frequently used in Scripture to express not only divine blessings, but these very blessings that are yet in store for the Church. See Isa. 44 : 3, &c.; Ezekiel's vision of the river flowing forth from the temple, ch. 47 ; Joel 3 : 18, and Rev. 22 : 1. To an Oriental in his burning clime, the image of a gushing stream,

9 And the LORD shall be King   there be one LORD, and his name
over all the earth : in that day shall   one.

whose grassy margin was overhung by waving trees, was
one of the most significant that could be used to express
a divine blessing. Their going out from Jerusalem, implied that the Church should be the medium of these
blessings ; their flowing to the Eastern and Western seas,
i. e. the Dead and Mediterranean, implied their universality, as these were the limits of the holy land ; whilst
their perennial endurance is declared by the fact that
they would be unaffected by either the summer's drought
or the winter's cold.

V. 9. "And Jehovah shall be king over the whole land, in that
day Jehovah shall be one, and his name one."

V. 9 explains this blessing in more distinct terms. It
shall consist in the acknowledgment of God's rightful
authority. Hitherto men have revolted from the one
God, and served divers lusts and vanities, and made to
themselves gods many and lords many. But then they
shall acknowledge God as their rightful ruler, and all
acknowledge the same God, know God by the same
name, and worship him with the same views. This
seems to be the meaning of the words, "Jehovah shall
be one and his name one." The diversities of the present shall give place to a living and glorious unity. This
is as if in designed denunciation of the type that infidelity is now assuming, that all existing forms of religion are
good, and that it is bigotry to assert any one only true
system of religious belief and practice. Henderson ren-

10 All the land shall be turned as a plain from Geba to Rimmon, south of Jerusalem : and it shall be lifted up, and inhabited in her place, from Benjamin's gate unto the place of the first gate, unto the corner gate, and *from* the tower of Hananeel unto the king's wine-presses.

ders the second clause " In that day Jehovah alone shall be, and his name alone," objecting that the other translation implies that before that day Jehovah was not one. But the same objection may be urged to his own translation, that it implies that before that day Jehovah did not exist alone.   In either case something must be supplied, and there is really but little to choose between the translations.

V. 10. "All the land shall be changed, as the plain from Geba to Rimmon, south of Jerusalem, and she shall be exalted and sit in her place, from the gate of Benjamin to the place of the first gate, to the gate of the corner, and from the tower of Hananeel to the king's wine-presses."

V. 10 describes symbolically the future exaltation and restoration of the Church.   This is described first by the prediction that all the mountainous region round about Jerusalem should be levelled into a plain, like the plain or valley of the Jordan.   " From Geba to Rimmon," expresses the fact that this would be general, as Geba was the northern limit of Judah (2 Kings 23 : 8), and Rimmon (not the rock Rimmon, but Rimmon of Simeon, Josh. 15 : 32,) was the southern.   The fact predicted is, not that the Church should be exalted so much as that the world should be humbled ; the cold and stony pride that has hitherto surrounded the Church should be abased, and that Church left in her lofty pre-eminence as the dwelling-place of God among men.

11 And *men* shall dwell in it, and there shall be no more utter destruction ; but Jerusalem shall be safely inhabited.

12 ¶ And this shall be the plague wherewith the LORD will smite all the people that have fought against Jerusalem ; Their flesh shall consume away while they stand upon their feet, and their eyes shall consume away in their holes, and their tongues shall consume away in their mouth.

The future restoration of the Church to her former condition is described by the terms, "From the gate of Benjamin to the place of the first gate," &c. This refers to the capture and sack described in v. 2, and declares that all trace of this destruction shall be effaced. The places named here are the boundaries of the city as they were known in the time of Zechariah, the gate of Benjamin being on the north, the first gate on the east, the tower of Hananeel on the south-east, the wine vats on the south-west, and the corner gate on the extreme west. The general fact predicted is that all traces of this time of trouble should be effaced, and the Church restored to all her former glory.

V. 11. " And they dwell in her, and there shall be no more curse, and Jerusalem sits in security."

V. 11 declares that there should be no return of these seasons of trial. Being kept pure, she needed not again to pass through the furnace, the days of her mourning being ended.

V. 12—15. " And this shall be the plague, with which Jehovah shall plague all nations which warred against Jerusalem ; his flesh shall rot, and he standing on his feet, and his eyes shall rot in their sockets, and their tongue shall rot in their mouth. And it shall be in that day there shall be among them a great confusion from Jehovah, and they shall seize each man the hand of his neighbor, and his hand shall rise against the hand of his neighbor. And Judah also shall fight in Jerusalem, and the wealth of

13 And it shall come to pass in that day, *that* a great tumult from the LORD shall be among them; and they shall lay hold every one on the hand of his neighbor, and his hand shall rise up against the hand of his neighbor.

14 And Judah also shall fight at Jerusalem; and the wealth of all the all the nations round about shall be gathered; gold, and silver, and garments in great abundance. And so shall be the plague of the horse, the mule, the camel, and the ass, which shall be in these camps, as this plague."

V. 12 introduces the declaration of the punishment that God would inflict on his enemies. This passage is parallel to Isa. 66 : 24, and seems to allude to the same general facts. It is a figurative description of the punishment of sin. The first element of the punishment is *corruption*, which is set forth by the terrible image of a living death, a fearful, anomalous state, in which the mouldy rottenness of death is combined in horrible union with the vivid, conscious sensibility of life. The soul of the sinner, in its future consciousness of sin, shall feel its loathsome corruption as vividly as now it would feel the slow putrefaction of the body that rotted piece-meal to the grave.

The second element of the punishment is given in v. 13, viz. : *mutual hate and contention.* The image is that of a panic-struck army, in which each man clutches and strikes in frantic fury his nearest neighbor. Hell shall be hate, in its fiercest and hatefullest forms. Sin is now the cause of all the quarrels on earth ; it shall be the cause of endless quarrels in hell. Oh, the thought of an everlasting scene of rage, hate, and conflict is intolerable ! and yet this is but sin left to itself.

heathen round about shall be gathered together, gold, and silver, and apparel, in great abundance.

15 And so shall be the plague of the

horse, of the mule, of the camel, and of the ass, and of all the beasts that shall be in these tents, as this plague.

16 ¶ And it shall come to pass, *that*

The third element of this punishment is given in v. 14, viz.: *loss of the blessings previously enjoyed.* This is represented by the image of spoil. The wealth of the nations that besieged Jerusalem shall be taken by Judah and Jerusalem, which are here combined in the triumph, as they were combined in the struggle described in ch. 12. This is parallel to the fact alluded to in the parable where the one talent is taken from the unfaithful servant and given to him who has ten talents. The blessings that sinners now have, and abuse in having, will then be taken from them and given to others.

ב after verbs of fighting generally means "*against*," but there are undoubted instances in which it has its natural meaning "in," (see Judges 5 : 19,) and hence it may be so rendered here without impropriety.

A fourth element is described in v. 15, viz.: *the infectious nature of sin.* Sin defiles all that it touches. It has defiled the earth and all it contains, so that it must be burned up; and it will hereafter transform the dwelling-place of its possessors into a hell, and their companions into fiends, and make it necessary that the very instruments of enjoyment they have possessed in life should be taken from them and destroyed.

These denunciations of punishment may refer to events preceding the last judgment, but they will not

every one that is left of all the nations which came against Jerusalem, shall even go up from year to year to worship the King, the LORD of hosts, and to keep the feast of tabernacles.

probably have their complete fulfilment until afterwards, when sin shall have developed itself perfectly into sorrow and everlasting woe.

V. 16. " And it shall be that the remnant of all the nations who came up against Jerusalem, shall go up from year to year, (*to Jerusalem*,) to worship the king, Jehovah of Hosts, and to keep the feast of tabernacles."

V. 16 turns to the Church, and asserts her supremacy over all her enemies, and her extension over all the earth.   This is done by the statement that all that survive of the nations of the earth shall come up to the observance of the feast of tabernacles.   This is of course not to be taken literally, as it would be impossible as a literal fact, without a miracle, and in contradiction to the obvious teachings of Paul in regard to the temporary character of these ordinances.   The feast of tabernacles was selected as the ground of this figurative prediction, because it was a feast of peculiar joy.   It was instituted as a memorial of the wanderings in the wilderness, and as an acknowledgment of the ingathering of the harvest.   It therefore clustered around it the memories of the past and the blessings of the present. The selection of it as a basis of the representation of future blessings to the Church implies, that in that period predicted her wanderings in the wilderness shall have ended, her seed-time of tears shall have issued in a reaping time of joy, and along the hills of light that

17 And it shall be, *that* whoso will not come up of *all* the families of the earth unto Jerusalem to worship the King, the LORD of hosts, even upon them shall be no rain.

stretch away in the Canaan above, there shall roll the everlasting song of her harvest home.

Henderson interprets this prediction literally, but perceiving the impossibility of all nations coming up to Jerusalem in mass, he makes them come up by representatives, which is of course to depart from the letter. There is, however, no more reason to take this literally, than to take other statements of the chapters, such as vs. 4, 5, 7, 8, &c., which are confessedly to be taken in a metaphorical sense. The future of the Theocracy or Church, is predicted under the forms and facts of the time when the prediction was made.

V. 17. "And it shall be that whoever of the tribes of the earth, will not go up to Jerusalem to worship the king, Jehovah of Hosts, upon them there shall be no rain."

V. 17 threatens that upon those who refuse to go up, there shall be no rain. It is not meant to be implied, that at the time predicted there shall be such disobedient persons, for in v. 16 it is clearly implied that there shall be none of such. It is rather a figurative assertion of the fact that, in this future condition, the present mingled state of reward and punishment shall end. Now God sends rain on the just and the unjust, then he will separate the good and the evil, and render unto every man according to his works.

V. 18. "And if the family of Egypt will not go forth, and come up, and there shall not be upon them (*therefore any rain,*) there

18. And if the family of Egypt go not up, and come not, that *have* no *rain;* there shall be the plague, where-

with the LORD will smite the heathen that come not up to keep the feast of tabernacles.

shall be the plague with which Jehovah shall plague the nations that do not come up to keep the feast of tabernacles."

V. 18 amplifies this thought. It might be thought that to some this threatening would convey nothing that they would fear, just as the threatening of no rain would not be feared by Egypt, which in fact rarely had any rain, but depended for water on the Nile. Thus to threaten a hardened sinner with the withholding of the gentle showers of divine grace, would seem to him to be no punishment, for he never had enjoyed these showers from heaven, but found his enjoyment in the turbid waters of the earthly. It is then declared that even for such, there shall be a suitable punishment, and one that they shall feel. God's magazine of wrath has an instrument for every shade of guilt. They who fear not the drought, shall tremble before the pestilence. The somewhat obscure words, וְלֹא עֲלֵיהֶם we have taken as expressing the result of the supposed disobedience, as threatened in v. 17. If Egypt refuses to obey, and as a consequence of this refusal there falls no rain upon her people, then although this would be no punishment to be dreaded by them, there shall be a punishment which they must dread; namely the plague. Some inter-preters supply " the Nile," and make this a prediction, that the Nile should not overflow. But this is very forced, and we naturally expect that such an ellipsis will be supplied, if possible, by some word already used,

19. This shall be the punishment of   nations that come not up to keep the
Egypt, and the punishment of all   feast of tabernacles.

which in this case is obviously the word "rain," which
gives a clear and consistent sense.

V. 19. "And this will be the sin of Egypt and the sin of all nations,
that come not up to keep the feast of tabernacles."

V. 19 explains what is the real nature of the sin of
the impenitent world, namely, a refusal to attach themselves to the people of God. It is therefore only a figurative declaration of the fact that unbelief and being
ashamed of Christ are the damning sins of the world.

Henderson takes the word "*sin*" here in the sense of
"punishment," and the verse as declaring that this is
the punishment of disobedient nations, but that makes
the verse a tautology.

V. 20, 21. "In that day there shall be upon the bells of the
horses 'Sacred to Jehovah.' And the vessels in the house of Jehovah shall be as the sacrificial bowls upon the altar. And every
vessel in Jerusalem and Judah shall be Sacred to Jehovah of
Hosts. And all the sacrificers shall come, and take from them
and offer in them, and there shall be no more a Canaanite in the
house of Jehovah of Hosts, in that day."

V. 20, 21, closes up this picture of the future with a
fitting finale, developing the great fact that this future
state of the Church would be happy because it would
be holy, and that this holiness would extend to everything connected with her. The distinction between
sacred and profane was introduced by sin, and would
cease with its termination on the earth. The Mosaic
dispensations drew the line with much sharpness and
narrowness; the Christian dispensation widened the

20 ¶ In that day there shall be upon the bells of the horses, HOLINESS UNTO THE LORD; and the pots in the LORD's house shall be like the bowls before the altar.

21 Yea, every pot in Jerusalem and

limits, and made all the saints to be priests, but there comes a time when this consecration shall be wider still, and extend to the minutest things pertaining to life. The "bells of the horses" were those bells that were fastened to them partly for ornament and partly to make them easily found if they strayed away at night. They were not necessary parts of the harness, and trifling in value. When, therefore, it is said that even they should have the inscription that was engraved on the breastplate of the high priest, this declares the fact that even the most trifling things in this future state of the Church should be consecrated to God, equally with the highest and holiest.

It is further stated that the vessels in the temple used for boiling, receiving ashes, &c., shall be as holy as the golden bowls that were used to catch the blood of the sacrificial victim. This is to affirm that all outward distinctions in the Church, official and otherwise, should be swallowed up in the great brotherhood of the children of God.

To show the extent of this holiness, it is added that the very cooking utensils of Jerusalem should be holy to the Lord, or that the smallest acts of the daily life should be consecrated, and holiness diffuse itself in living power through the whole man, in all the departments of his activity, leading him whatsoever he does to

in Judah shall be holiness unto the Lord of hosts : and all they that sacrifice shall come and take of them, and seethe therein : and in that day there shall be no more the Canaanite in the house of the Lord of hosts.

do all to the glory of God. The idea is, absolute and universal consecration to the Lord.

The words " all the sacrificers shall come," &c., imply that this condition shall be one of active obedience, and not of mere passive enjoyment ; whilst the prediction that there should be no more a Canaanite in the house of the Lord, affirms that no profane or unclean person shall there be found in the redeemed Church. Most of the expositors take " Canaanite " here to mean " merchant," as it sometimes does. But there is no necessity for thus restricting its meaning. It was to the Jew the type of an alien, and here predicts that the mingled condition of the present shall give place to a state in the future in which all shall be holy, and nothing unclean be found in the new Jerusalem. The whole passage is then parallel with the sublime close of the Apocalypse, in which the holiness of the heavenly state is depicted in such magnificent terms. All shall be happy because all shall be holy. Sorrow shall cease because sin shall cease. The groaning earth shall be mantled with joy because the trail of the serpent shall be gone, and the Eden of the future make us cease to look back with longing at the Eden of the past. If then a man would have the beginnings of Heaven, it must be by this absolute consecration of everything to God on earth, for precisely as " holiness to the Lord " is upon the "bells of the horses," shall their melody have the ring of the golden harps. Let a man's life be a liturgy, a holy service of acted worship, and his death shall be a sweeter melody than the fabled song of the dying swan, and his eternity the song of Moses and the Lamb.

PRACTICAL INFERENCES.

(1.) There are scenes of trouble yet before the Church of the most appalling character. There is as much necessity for such scenes now, as there ever has been in the past. The divisions of Christians into sects, parties, and cliques, the alienation often of brother from brother, has made the Church, not like a mass of pure gold, ready for the fashioning workman, but like a mass of ore, cold, earthy, dim and defiled, ready for the furnace. Let this ore be cast into the furnace, and the dross will be purged out, the pure metal flow together in bright and beautiful blendings, and the gold come forth seven times refined. Hence, as we read the promises of future purity and power, we cannot see how they can so well be fulfilled as by purging with fire. And as we look at the troubled state of political affairs, and the menacing aspects of Popery and Infidelity, we can readily see how this may soon happen, (v. 1, 2.)

(2.) When the Church's greatest need shall come, then shall come God's greatest deliverance, so that we need not fear, Ps. 45, (v. 3—5.)

(3.) Christ is coming to the earth, in such form at

least as shall fulfil his purposes of mercy to his friends and justice to his foes, (v. 5.)

(4.) However dark the day, in the Christian life, at evening time there shall be light.   His life is a twilight, but it is the twilight of the morning, that shall brighten and broaden into a day that has neither sunset nor night ; whilst the twilight of the sinner is that of the evening, that shall thicken and blacken into that long and gloomy night that knows no morning, (v. 7.)

(5.) There is but one way of salvation, one object of worship, and one Mediator, (v. 9.)

(6.) In the future glory of the Church the mountains of imaginary causes that now separate Christians shall vanish, and they all see eye to eye, and be *one*, even as their God and Saviour, (v. 10.)

(7.) The most fearful punishment of sinners is simply to leave them to themselves.   Sin is but hell in embryo, hell is but sin in development, (v. 12—15.)

(8.) God has a scourge fitted for every sin, and all shall receive precisely as they have deserved, (v. 18.)

(9.) When there shall be universal holiness, there shall also be universal happiness, (v. 20, 21.)

As the depth of meaning contained in the last three chapters of this prophecy is far from being exhausted by any one commentator, and as there are differences of opinion on points of no small importance, it will probably be found helpful to include here some quotations from other writers. These will serve to supplement Moore's exegesis and in general to substantiate his views.

There is widespread agreement among expositors concerning Chapter 11. It describes Israel's rejection of the Good Shepherd, the Messiah, and their consequent punishment as a nation. Dr. Talbot Chambers (in Lange's Commentaries on the Holy Scriptures) gives the following helpful analysis of that chapter: "The first three verses describe the ruin of the entire land . . . Then the cause of this widespread desolation is set forth, not by vision as in the earlier portion, but by symbolical action or process subjectively wrought. Israel is a flock doomed to perish by the divine judgment. The Prophet, personating his Lord, makes an effort to avert the threatened infliction. He therefore assumes the office of shepherd, equipped with staves fitted to secure success. He seeks to rid them of false leaders, and win .them to ways of truth and right. But the attempt is vain, because of their obdurate

* Inserted by the Publishers of this 1958 reprint of Moore's commentary.

wickedness, and the issue is a mutual recoil. He loathes them; they abhor him. Accordingly he significantly breaks his staves in token that all is over. But after breaking one, and before doing the same to the other, the shepherd asks a reward for his unavailing effort. He receives one, but it is so trifling that he had better have received none. They insult him with the offer of the price of a slave (vv. 4–14). Then the scene changes. Instead of a wise, kind shepherd, the Prophet personates one of an opposite character . . . The flock, so far from being fed and guided and guarded, is torn and devoured, and then at last its misguided rulers are smitten and palsied, and so the curtain falls (vv. 15–17)."

Whether Israel is ever again spoken of as a nation in the next three chapters is perhaps the first point at issue. Chambers is a good representative of the opinion that it is not. "The Prophet here passes," he says in his introduction to Chapters 12–14, "from the old to the new form of the Church, he refers to the Kingdom of God on earth after the appearance of the Messiah, and describes its trials and triumphs, its inward and outward development . . . The Christian Church is the legitimate continuation of the Old Testament Israel. There is but one Israel, one people of God from the beginning to the end. According to the Apostle's figure, old branches were broken off and new ones grafted on, but there was only the one olive tree throughout. Gentiles when they come to Christ,

are incorporated into the commonwealth of Israel, so
as to become fellow-citizens with the saints, i.e. those
who are already such (Eph. 2. 12–19). It is one and
the same body, differing in outward and unessential
characteristics, but maintaining an unbroken identity
in all that belongs to substance and life." Accordingly
Chambers gives this summary of the leading themes
in the closing chapters: "The victory of God's Kingdom over the heathen world (12. 1–9), the repentance
and conversion of the children of the Kingdom (12. 10;
13. 1), their purification from all ungodliness (13. 2–6),
a severe sifting of the flock consequent upon the smiting of the shepherd (13. 7–9), and the final tremendous
conflict of the Church and the world, ending in the
assured victory of the former (Ch. 14)."

The first nine verses of Chapter 12 Chambers does
not view as describing specific events; they were
fulfilled not only in the bloody onslaught of pagan
power on the infant Church and in the Church's
victory over the first ten persecutions, but also in
"Christian Israel's conflicts with the world's power as
they are renewed from age to age." He relates the
second section in Chapter 12, beginning at v. 9, to
the preceding in the following way: "As the former
portion of the chapter set forth the outward protection of Providence shown toward the New Testament
Israel, by means of which it emerged victor from all
trials and conflicts, and saw its enemies utterly dis-
comfited, this portion turns to the other side of

Israel's experience and deals with its inward character, showing how the covenant people become such,
how the Church in its new form commences the
Christian life, and obtains a title to the divine protection. It is by the bitter herbs of repentance,
leading to pardon and renovation through a believing
sight of the pierced Saviour . . . In this view the two
parts of the chapter correspond to each other and
make one complete whole. The result of the failure
of the shepherd in Ch. 11 is shown to be not final and
absolute, but a link in the chain of events which
works out the fulfilment of the old covenant promises,
and the ingathering of all the Israel of God."

In dealing with Ch. 13. 2–6, and with the opening
verses of Ch. 14, Chambers likewise regards the
picture as describing events that would have a continuous fulfilment throughout the Christian era rather
than having a specific and literal character. On
Ch. 13. 2–6, he comments, "The passage is not to be
restricted to any particular period, but describes
under local and temporary forms the removal of
whatever is offensive to a God of holiness and truth.
It will therefore apply to every instance in which the
Gospel in its leading elements is truly received." In
dealing with Ch. 14 he asserts the figurative nature of
the language—a principle with which all sound commentators are largely agreed. "The cleaving of the
Mount of Olives in two for the purpose of affording
escape to fugitives from Jerusalem; the flowing of

two perpetual streams from the holy city in opposite directions; the levelling of the whole land in order to exalt the temple-mountain; the yearly pilgrimage of all nations of the earth to Jerusalem; and the renewal of the old sacrifices of the Mosaic ritual; these are plainly symbolical statements." He then proceeds to state his inclination to regard the description of conflict with which the passage opens "as an ideal picture of all the conflicts of the Church with its foes . . . from the beginning to the end of the Christian dispensation. Prophecy was never intended to be history written in advance . . . But the broad outlines which defy literal explanation, yet serve to indicate great principles, and disclose the springs of God's moral government." It can thus be seen that Chambers — and others whose views he serves to represent—differs from Moore in two respects.

(1) Moore, while avoiding the extravagant literalism of some modern writers who would exclude the Christian Church altogether from these chapters, regards this portion of Scripture as containing evidence of a future spiritual work among the Jews as a people. Zechariah traces, he says, "the historic course of the covenant people down to the time when the unbelieving Jewish element was to be eliminated, and onward to the period when it should be restored." The great spiritual blessing promised in Ch. 12. 10–14, is "contemplated mainly as now containing the peni-

tent Jews"; and "the great revival of the future" pictured in Ch. 13. 1–6, "will restore the Jews to the church from which they had been so long separated by unbelief." The third part who will be brought through the fire (Ch. 13. 9), "includes not only the Jews who were converted to Christianity, and who passed through the fires of persecution, but also that portion that survived the dispersion and still remain in unbelief" . . . and the verses thus show that "there are yet purposes of mercy in reserve for the ancient covenant people".

While agreeing with Chambers that it is generally right to regard the Church as the New Testament Israel, we are, like Moore, not satisfied that the meaning of these closing chapters of Zechariah can be fully explained in that way. The question turns perhaps on how far we are prepared to see evidence for a future conversion of the Jews in other Scriptures, such as Romans, Ch. 11, and passages of Ezekiel and Isaiah. An interpretation of these other Scriptures is obviously outside the scope of this present appendix. There are worthy expositors on both sides, and the question can never be decided by an appeal to names, but it may be of interest to mention a few who would endorse Moore's position. George Hutcheson, the eminent Scottish expositor of the seventeenth century in his introduction to Zechariah, Ch. 12, writes, "The Lord subjoins many comfortable promises in this chapter, which however they have their own accomplishment, and yield comfort to the Israel of God in all woes, yet the full accomplishment of them is reserved for converted Israel." On verse 12 of the same chapter he comments, "The conversion of the Jews or Israel unto the Messiah, is not to be of some few only, but national of the body of that people, and there will be real repentance among many of them." Probably the majority of the English Puritans held the same position as Hutcheson. William Greenhill, for instance, expounding Ezekiel 37. 22-24, declares, "This conversion of the Jews will be not of some few particulars, but national, though not of every one belonging to the nation." Thomas Boston, the eighteenth-century Scottish evangelical leader, in a sermon on Zech. 12. 12, refers to Rom. 11. 25-36 as a parallel passage, in which verses, he says, the apostle Paul "shews that the blindness of the Jews is only in part, and to last only to a certain time, when there shall be a national conversion, and so all Israel shall be saved. This is not meant of the spiritual Israel, for their conversion could be no mystery as this is. But as the conversion of the Gentiles was a mystery to the Jews, and to Gentiles themselves under the Old Testament, Eph. 3. 3-6, so is that of the Jews to the Gentiles and Jews themselves, under the New Testament. And as many Jews then would not believe the one, so many Christians now believe not the other." Charles Hodge, in a section on "The Conversion of the Jews" in his great "Systematic

Theology", likewise refers to Zech. 12. 12 as one of
the "express predictions of their national conversion
to faith in Him whom they had rejected and crucified".

(2) The second major difference between Moore and
Chambers is also one which has divided the best
commentators and relates to the time and manner of
the fulfilment of these chapters. Naturally one's
judgment on this question will be largely governed
by the view taken of the first difference. If these
chapters are believed to contain predictions of a
widespread spiritual work amongst the Jews, then
they are yet unfulfilled and must refer to a period
yet future.

This difference however is not so radical as might
first appear, and it is possible to accommodate the
two views. Chambers, Hengstenberg, and others have
much to support their opinion that the language of
these chapters is symbolical. It was never, they say,
intended to refer to one or two particular historical
events, but rather it describes in general terms the
whole development of the Messianic era to its close.
There is reason to believe such language is used in
other parts of Scripture, e.g. the Book of Revelation,
where, for instance, the trumpets of judgment do not
symbolize separate and single events but calamities
which will occur again and again throughout this
dispensation. (Cf. W. Hendriksen's commentary on
the Book of Revelation, entitled "More Than Con-

querors"). Keil ably expounds this view of a continuous fulfilment but also indicates how this still
leaves room for regarding the final and complete
fulfilment as yet future. Commenting on Zechariah
12. 10, "They shall look upon me whom they have
pierced", he writes, "The historical fulfilment of this
prophecy commenced with the crucifixion of the Son
of God. The words are quoted in the Gospel of John
(xix. 37) as having been fulfilled in Christ, by the fact
that a soldier pierced His side with a lance as He was
hanging upon the cross (*vide* John xix. 34). . . . There
can be no doubt that John quotes this passage with
distinct allusion to this special circumstance; only
we must not infer from this, that the evangelist
regarded the meaning of the prophecy as exhausted
by this allusion . . . The true and full commencement
of the fulfilment shows itself in the success which
attended the preaching of Peter on the first day of
Pentecost, and in the further results which followed
the preaching of the apostles for the conversion of
Israel (Acts iii–v). The fulfilment has continued with
less striking results through the whole period of the
Christian Church, in conversions from among the
Jews; and it will not terminate till the remnant of
Israel shall turn as a people to Jesus the Messiah,
whom its fathers crucified." (Commentary on the
Minor Prophets, Keil and Delitzsch, vol. 2.) Keil
treats Ch. 12. 1–9 in the same manner, "As the
believing penitential look at the pierced One will not

take place for the first time at the ultimate conversion of Israel at the end of the days, so did the siege of Jerusalem by all nations, i.e. the attack of the heathen nations upon the Church of God, commence even in the days of the apostles (cf. Acts iv. 25 *sqq.*), and continues through the whole history of the Christian Church to the last great conflict which will immediately precede the return of our Lord to judgment." Likewise on Ch. 14. 1–5, "This issue takes place, no doubt, only at the end of the course of this world, with the return of Christ to the last judgment; but the fact that Jerusalem is conquered and plundered, and the half of its population led away into captivity, proves indisputably that the siege of Jerusalem predicted in Ch. xiv must not be restricted to the last attack of Antichrist upon the church of the Lord, but that all the hostile attacks of the heathen world upon the city of God are embraced in the one picture of a siege of Jerusalem. In the attack made upon Jerusalem by Gog and Magog, the city is not conquered and plundered, either according to Ezek. xxxviii and xxxix, or according to Rev. xx. 7–9; but the enemy is destroyed by the immediate interposition of the Lord, without having got possession of the holy city. But to this ideal summary of the conflicts and victories of the nations of the world there is appended directly the picture of the final destruction of the ungodly power of the world, and the glorification of the Kingdom of God; so that in

Ch. xiv (from vv. 6–12) there is predicted in Old Testament form the completion of the Kingdom of God, which the Apostle John saw and described in Rev. xx–xxii in New Testament mode under the figure of the heavenly Jerusalem."

We have only attempted to summarize briefly some of the general views taken of these closing chapters and have not entered into details. There are however one or two points of difference in the exegesis of particular verses in Ch. 14 that will influence our interpretation of the whole. In v. 1 Moore expounds "thy spoil" to be the spoil taken by the Church, thus indicating the triumph of God's people. But the majority understand the phrase to mean not the booty which the city takes, but that which is taken from her and in a leisurely manner divided among her conquerors. Keil thus asserts that it is the same picture as in Ch. 12. 2–9; "These passages", he says, "do not treat of two different attacks upon the Church of God, occurring at different times; but, whilst Ch. xii depicts the constantly repeated attack in the light of its successful overthrow, Ch. xiv describes the hostile attack according to its partial success and final issue in the destruction of the powers that are hostile to God." This view, if it is correct, makes little difference to Moore's over-all picture.

Moore does not take the intervention of God, described in vv. 4–5 of Ch. 14, as referring to the

Final Judgment Day, and interprets vv. 6–7 as a period between that intervention and Christ's Second Coming when "at evening time it shall be light". The phrase "not day, not night" he understands as meaning a phrase of twilight dimness. Others however do not expound vv. 6–7 as referring to a different period, but take the verses as a varied description of the same Coming spoken of in v. 4. "Not day and not night", they say, does not mean an admixture of both, but neither; a time when there would be no means of determining what is day and what night because the lights of heaven would be put out, and the whole order of nature miraculously reversed. The language is therefore the same as in other prophetic announcements of the day of judgment. (Matt. 24. 29; Rev. 6. 12 etc.)

A difficulty in the view that vv. 8–21 describe the glorious and perfect condition of the Church of God and the utter and complete destruction of her enemies after Christ's Coming, lies in the apparent suggestion in v. 17 that at this time there would still be some ungodly. But, says Moore, "it is not meant to be implied, that at the time predicted there shall be such disobedient persons, for in v. 16 it is clearly implied that there shall be none of such". With this Keil agrees. "We must not infer", from vv. 17–19, "that at the time of the completion of the Kingdom of God there will still be heathen, who will abstain from the worship of the true God; but the thought is simply this: there will then be no more room for heathenism within the sphere of the Kingdom of God. To this there is appended the thought, in vv. 20–21, that everything unholy will then be removed from that Kingdom." As Moore says, the complete fulfilment of these denunciations of punishment refers most probably to the time after Christ's Second Coming when, in Hell, "sin shall have developed itself perfectly into sorrow and everlasting woe".

May these chapters be used to show us more of the present darkness of our minds, the smallness of our understandings, the brevity of time and the uncertainty of all earthly prospects, that we—like the Old Testament saints—may be led to "desire a better country, that is, an heavenly"! (Heb. 11. 16.)